SUPPORTING CAPITAL MARKET DEVELOPMENT AND REFORM

COUNTRY ASSESSMENT REPORT FOR MONGOLIA

DECEMBER 2025

ASIAN DEVELOPMENT BANK

ADB

6 ADB Avenue, Mandaluyong City, 1550 Metro Manila, Philippines
Tel +63 2 8632 4444; Fax +63 2 8636 2444
www.adb.org

ISBN 978-92-9277-632-9 (print); 978-92-9277-633-6 (PDF); 978-92-9277-634-3 (ebook)
Publication Stock No. TCS250561-2
DOI: http://dx.doi.org/10.22617/TCS250561-2

Note:
In this publication, "$" refers to United States dollars.

Cover design by Cleone Flores Baradas.

On the cover (clockwise from top left): (i) a construction worker of a railway station in Viet Nam, (ii) engineers and technicians of a power plant in Uzbekistan, (iii) beneficiaries of an electricity grid development program in Indonesia, (iv) various currency symbols (designed by Claudette Rodrigo), (v) ADB headquarters building in Manila, and (vi) stock market analysis chart (www.freepik.com). All other photos by ADB.

CONTENTS

TABLES AND FIGURES

TABLES

FIGURES

ACKNOWLEDGMENTS

As the acting senior director of the Finance Sector Office (SD3-FIN) at the Asian Development Bank (ADB), I would like to extend my profound gratitude to the TA 6716–REG research team (lead consultant Kim Pil-Kyu, international consultant Ki-Hoon Ro, and national consultant Bilguun Dashdorj), and staff for their continuous support and guidance throughout the entire period of this study.

In particular, I would also like to express my sincere appreciation to the Ministry of Finance of Mongolia, the financial market infrastructures, and the participants of the Mongolian local currency bond market (LCBM). Without their dedicated assistance, timely support, and constructive feedback, we would not have been able to complete this work efficiently.

Kyung Soo Shin, finance sector specialist, SD3-FIN led the efforts to coordinate and contribute to the development and production of the publication. The publication also greatly benefited from comments received from Arup Chatterjee, Edward Faber, and Peter Rosenkranz in the SD3-FIN.

This publication analyzed the status of the legal and regulatory framework, financial market infrastructures, investor base, issuer base, and intermediation, which are key components of the Mongolian LCBM, using ADB's standardized diagnostic methods. Through this analysis, we identified the factors hindering the development of the current LCBM and proposed measures to overcome these challenges and promote its growth. We sincerely hope that these recommendations will contribute to the development of the Mongolian LCBM.

ADB pledges to continue its efforts in developing infrastructure for the financial market, including the bond market, in the Asia and Pacific region.

The publication was produced with the support of Katherine Mitzi Co, operations analyst, SD3-FIN. Consultant Ma. Kristina Mahilum provided valuable administrative support.

This publication does not represent the official views of ADB or any of the institutions mentioned herein.

Tariq Niazi
Officer-in-Charge, Senior Director, SD3-FIN, Sectors Department 3
Asian Development Bank

ABBREVIATIONS

ABS	asset-backed securities
ADB	Asian Development Bank
BOM	Bank of Mongolia
CCP	central counterparty
CIS	collective investment scheme
CRA	credit rating agency
CSD	Central Securities Depository
DMC	developing member country
DVP	delivery versus payment
EFF	Extended Fund Facility
FMI	financial market infrastructure
FRC	Financial Regulatory Commission
GDP	gross domestic product
GSS	green, social, and sustainability
IMF	International Monetary Fund
IOSCO	International Organization of Securities Commissions
LCBM	local currency bond market
LLC	limited liability company
MASD	Mongolian Association of Securities Dealers
MCSD	Mongolian Central Securities Depository
MNT	Mongolian togrog
MOF	Ministry of Finance
MSCC	Mongolian Securities Clearing Center
MSCH&CD	Mongolian Securities Clearing House and Central Depository
MSE	Mongolian Stock Exchange
OTC	over-the-counter
PFMI	Principles for Financial Market Infrastructures
SLB	Securities Lending and Borrowing
SRO	self-regulatory organization
SSS	securities settlement system

CURRENCY EQUIVALENTS (as of 30 June 2025)

Currency Unit		Mongolian togrog (MNT)
MNT1.00	=	$0.000279
$1.00	=	MNT3,580.94

EXECUTIVE SUMMARY

This country assessment reviews the capital market landscape and gaps in Mongolia, with a focus on the local currency bond market (LCBM). The assessment is based on *A Diagnostic Framework for Local Currency Bond Market* (2024) prepared by the Asian Development Bank. Within this framework, it reviews five dimensions relevant to developing LCBMs: legal and regulatory framework, financial market infrastructures (FMIs), investor base, issuer base, and intermediation.

Legal and Regulatory Framework

- **Key findings.** The bond market in Mongolia has witnessed significant regulatory advancements, such as the introduction of the Regulation on Debt Instrument Registration (2021) and the Regulation on Operation of the Over-the-Counter Market (2020). These regulations have streamlined the bond issuance process, established a framework for the over-the-counter (OTC) market, and paved the way for the issuance of green, social, and sustainability bonds. Additionally, amendments to the Securities Market Law, approved by legislators on 16 May 2024, aim to update the law to reflect recent developments in the market. These include differentiating between exchange and OTC markets, supporting collective investment schemes, paving the way for international financial institutions to issue bonds on the Mongolian capital market, and simplifying the process for underwriters to issue securities in a public offering. Challenges persist, however. These include the lack of explicit provisions for bond defaults and bondholders' representatives, potential conflicts of interest due to bond underwriters assuming the role of bondholders' representatives, inconsistencies between the Securities Market Law and Financial Regulatory Commission (FRC) regulations, and inefficiencies in clearing and settlement processes. Addressing these regulatory gaps and aligning with international best practices is crucial for fostering investor confidence and attracting domestic and foreign investment in the Mongolian bond market.
- **Recommendation 1: Further enhance the legal and regulatory framework to bolster mechanisms protecting investors, especially in default situations, and to streamline settlement processes and custody while maintaining regulatory flexibility.**
    - (i) Building on the amended Securities Market Law, the FRC regulations must be swiftly reorganized and refined. Specifically, clear and detailed procedures and provisions addressing both bond defaults and cross-default situations must be established. To ensure both regulatory consistency and practical effectiveness, international best practices from civil law jurisdictions such as France, Germany, and the Republic of Korea should be benchmarked and integrated.
    - (ii) Implement a regulatory framework to oversee the appointment and functioning of bondholders' representatives or trustees, particularly in bond default and cross-default scenarios, ensuring their actions align with the best interests of bondholders and international best practices. Establish clear separation between bond underwriters and bondholders' representatives or trustees to prevent conflicts of interest, with this separation enforced through regulatory guidelines that ensure fiduciary duties toward bondholders are not compromised.

(iii) Continue refining the operational frameworks of FMIs to fully implement the provisions of the amended Securities Market Law, particularly those related to clearing, settlement, and custody services.

(iv) Develop a comprehensive bond custodian regime aligned with the amended Securities Market Law that establishes clear custody arrangements facilitating cross-border investment flows, supports the creation of a government bond yield curve, and enables the development of a secondary market and instruments such as securities lending and repo.

(v) Review the regulatory framework for green, social, and sustainability bonds once sufficient market data is available to assess its effectiveness.

(vi) Clarify and strengthen the governance and oversight framework for self-regulatory organizations to ensure consistency in delegated regulatory functions and accountability aligned with international best practices.

(vii) Harmonize terminology in relevant laws and regulations to standardize the use of "bond" and align with international market conventions and investor expectations.

Financial Market Infrastructure

- **Key findings.** Upon evaluating the roles and functions of FMIs as outlined in the Principles for Financial Market Infrastructures (PFMI), it becomes evident that Mongolian FMIs have not fully established the requisite functions. Specifically, the legal frameworks for central counterparties and securities settlement systems are unclear and lacking essential features. The IT systems supporting central counterparties and securities settlement systems, implemented 18 years ago, are now outdated, raising concerns about system stability and the feasibility of integrating advanced risk management features, such as securities lending and borrowing. Meanwhile, the recent investment by the Bank of Mongolia in new IT infrastructure for central securities depository functions has been underutilized due to coordination gaps between institutions. This situation necessitates prompt resolution, as the core objective of FMIs is to minimize transaction costs, reduce risks, and enhance efficiency.
- **Recommendation 2: Develop a unified approach in advancing and implementing FMI systems to address coordination gaps and enhance operational effectiveness.**

  (i) Establish a specialized organization, tentatively named the "Capital Market Efficiency Committee," to plan and implement advancements in efficiency for post-trade settlement and clearing activities.

  (ii) Strengthen the coordination function of the Financial Market Stability Council to align national FMI modernization efforts and ensure regulatory coherence across FMIs and supervisory bodies.

  (iii) Bolster Mongolia's capital market infrastructure by supporting the Mongolian Central Securities Depository to either migrate to the Bank of Mongolia's DEPO/X system or develop/procure its own IT system to replace the outdated infrastructure, prioritizing the option that best serves long-term operational efficiency and customization needs.

  (iv) Review the introduction of a central counterparty system to efficiently manage credit risk in the capital market, including the adoption of legal frameworks and risk management systems aligned with the PFMI.

(v) Validate the effectiveness of the current delivery versus payment model and implement a delivery versus payment framework aligned with the PFMI to efficiently manage principal risk in the capital market.

(vi) Foster qualitative growth in Mongolia's capital market by reviewing the introduction of liquidity provision mechanisms such as securities lending and borrowing and tri-party repo, ensuring efficient implementation in conjunction with new IT system adoption.

Investor Base

- **Key findings.** Mongolia's investor base for bonds is underdeveloped. Pensions are part of the fiscal budget, private pension funds are nascent, the size of collective investment schemes is limited, and constraints in the insurance industry limit the potential for expanding the bond market investor base. In addition, limitations in post-trade services supporting bond trades of foreign investors, including the absence of international central securities depositories, combined with the country's low credit rating, mean that foreign investment is likely to remain limited in the near term. In the case of corporate bonds, the investor pool is predominantly high-net-worth individuals, with foreign investors discouraged by onerous paperwork and high withholding tax. Insufficient incentives and restrictive policies for insurance firms and pension funds further inhibit broader market participation.
- **Recommendation 3: Foster bond market development by expanding and diversifying the investor base.**

(i) Continue to leverage the amended Investment Fund Law and existing tax incentives to further develop diverse investor profiles, including collective investment schemes, asset management firms, and insurance companies, to expand the investment base for corporate bonds. This should involve revising regulatory hurdles that limit insurance company investments and updating pension fund regulations to encourage their engagement in the market.

(ii) Address the lack of foreign investors by simplifying procedural obligations and facilitating the entry of global custodians.

(iii) Clarify the regulatory definitions of "listing" and "registration" to eliminate confusion and revise restrictions that prevent mutual funds from accessing the OTC bond market.

(iv) Enhance financial literacy and retail investor education programs, with a focus on raising awareness and understanding of fixed-income instruments.

(v) Introduce a regulatory framework for bondholder representatives or trustees to strengthen investor protection in the bond market.

(vi) Develop the legal, operational, and risk management framework needed to implement omnibus accounts and connect the Mongolian Central Securities Depository to international central securities depositories such as Clearstream and Euroclear.

Issuer Base

- **Key findings.** Following the successful completion of the International Monetary Fund's Extended Fund Facility program, the government resumed issuing local currency bonds on 16 April 2025, in line with Goal 4 of the government's Medium-Term Debt Management Strategy 2023–2025. The new unified issuance system operates through the Mongolian Stock Exchange's electronic platform. Biweekly auctions are held across three maturity categories: short-term (up to 1 year), medium-term (1–5 years), and long-term (over 5 years). This addresses previous systemic weaknesses, including the dual-venue structure that resulted in different International Securities Identification Numbers for identical bonds, vulnerability to investor collusion, and the absence of a proper yield curve. Prior to resumption, the lack of government bonds forced corporate issuers to rely on commercial bank savings rates for pricing, limiting most corporate bond maturities to under 2 years. The corporate bond market has seen significant growth since the introduction of the professional-only OTC market in September 2021, with issuance times reduced to 1–2 weeks compared to 2–4 months for public offerings.

- **Recommendation 4: Optimize government bond market development and enhance market participation.**
  - (i) Focus on developing benchmark issues across the yield curve as the government bond market matures, ensuring sufficient liquidity in secondary markets and building fungible benchmark issues to enhance the market's utility as a pricing reference for corporate bonds.
  - (ii) Diversify the investor base for government bonds beyond commercial banks to include entities with varying risk appetites, such as mutual funds, pension funds, and insurance companies. Encourage securities companies to take an active role in developing repo markets and foster more active secondary trading to enhance overall market liquidity.
  - (iii) Promote regulatory certainty and continued support for OTC bond issuance to sustain access for issuers and reduce time-to-market, while maintaining investor protection standards.
  - (iv) Define "true sale" and "bankruptcy remoteness" under the Securities Market Law to provide a stable legal basis for securitization transactions in line with international practices.
  - (v) Support the development of credit rating agencies through capacity building, technical assistance, and implementation of rating quality standards to ensure meaningful and trusted credit assessments in the bond market.

Intermediation

- **Key findings.** The absence of a primary dealer system results in limited development of the secondary market for government bonds. In the corporate bond sector, legacy paper-based operations and inactive firms hinder market development. Only 15 brokerage firms participate in the OTC bond market, with only a handful having the capacity to invest in system upgrades and evolve with market developments. Out of 55 licensed brokerage firms, less than half are actively operating, creating barriers to transitioning to fully digital operations. This issue is compounded by the practice of requiring pre-funding for bond transactions. The MSE trading system, used for government bond issuance, cannot be updated as the system's foreign developer no longer exists and the MSE lacks the source code. In comparison, the locally developed M-OTC platform offers advantages including full digitalization and faster settlement times (T+0 or T+1), and it has become Mongolia's largest securities trading venue by volume.
- **Recommendation 5: Consider introducing a primary dealer system for government bonds and raise securities company qualification requirements.**
  - (i) Introduce a primary dealer system aligned with local market conditions to establish a secondary market for government bonds, improving the efficiency of issuance and trading in the Mongolian government bond market while generating a much-needed benchmark interest rate for the financial market.

(ii) Enhance intermediary credibility by introducing regulations that permit only investment banks with strong creditworthiness and technological capabilities to underwrite and broker corporate bonds. Reevaluate minimum capital requirements and accelerate the transition from paper-based processes through synchronized system enhancements across market participants.

(iii) Implement a tier-based licensing system for brokerage firms based on operational capabilities, capital adequacy, and technological readiness. Establish technical assistance programs for inactive firms and develop consolidation frameworks for firms unable to meet updated requirements.

(iv) Explore options to broaden retail investor access to OTC bond instruments, through mutual funds, investment platforms, or fintech channels.

(v) Establish a framework for reliable bond pricing using independent pricing services or credit rating agencies to strengthen transparency and investor confidence.

Recommendations for Capital Market Development in Mongolia

Recommendation	Agency	Timing[a]
Legal and regulatory framework		
1. Further enhance the legal and regulatory framework to bolster mechanisms protecting investors, especially in default situations, and to streamline settlement processes and custody while maintaining regulatory flexibility.		
(i) Building on the amended Securities Market Law, develop FRC regulations to provide more detailed provisions addressing bond defaults and cross-default situations, drawing on international examples from civil law jurisdictions such as France, Germany, and the Republic of Korea.	FRC	MT
(ii) Implement a regulatory framework to oversee the appointment and functioning of bondholders' representatives or trustees, particularly in bond default and cross-default scenarios, ensuring their actions align with the best interests of bondholders and international best practices. Establish clear separation between bond underwriters and bondholders' representatives or trustees to prevent conflicts of interest, with this separation enforced through regulatory guidelines that ensure fiduciary duties toward bondholders are not compromised.	FRC	MT
(iii) Continue refining the operational frameworks of financial market infrastructures to fully implement the provisions of the amended Securities Market Law, particularly those related to clearing, settlement, and custody services.	MOF, FRC, MCSD	NT
(iv) Develop a comprehensive bond custodian regime aligned with the amended Securities Market Law that establishes clear custody arrangements facilitating cross-border investment flows, support the creation of a government bond yield curve, and enable the development of a secondary market and instruments such as securities lending and repo.	MOF, FRC, MCSD	MT

continued on next page

Continued

Recommendation	Agency	Timing[a]
(v) Review the regulatory framework for green, social, and sustainability bonds once sufficient market data is available to assess its effectiveness.	FRC	MT
(vi) Clarify and strengthen the governance and oversight framework for self-regulatory organizations to ensure consistency in delegated regulatory functions and accountability aligned with international best practices.	FRC, MASD	NT
(vii) Harmonize terminology in relevant laws and regulations to standardize the use of "bond" and align with international market conventions and investor expectations.	MOF, FRC	NT
Financial market infrastructure		
2. Develop a unified approach for the advancement and implementation of financial market infrastructure systems to address coordination gaps and enhance operational effectiveness.		
(i) Establish a specialized organization, tentatively named the "Capital Market Efficiency Committee," to plan and implement advancements in efficiency for post-trade settlement and clearing activities.	MOF, FRC, BOM	NT
(ii) Strengthen the coordination function of the Financial Market Stability Council to align national FMI modernization efforts and ensure regulatory coherence across FMIs and supervisory bodies.	MOF, FRC, BOM	MT
(iii) Bolster capital market infrastructure by supporting the Mongolian Central Securities Depository to either migrate to the BOM's DEPO/X system or develop/procure its own IT system to replace the outdated central securities depository/securities settlement system infrastructure, prioritizing the option that best serves long-term operational efficiency and customization needs.	MOF, FRC, BOM, MCSD, MSCC	MT
(iv) Review the introduction of a central counterparty system to efficiently manage credit risk in the capital market, including the adoption of legal frameworks and risk management systems aligned with the Principles for Financial Market Infrastructures.	MOF, FRC, MSCC	MT
(v) Validate the effectiveness of the current delivery versus payment model and implement a delivery versus payment framework aligned with the Principles for Financial Market Infrastructures to efficiently manage principal risk in the capital market.	MOF, FRC, MCSD, MSCC	NT
(vi) Foster qualitative growth in Mongolia's capital market by considering the introduction of liquidity provision mechanisms such as securities lending and borrowing and tri-party repo, ensuring efficient implementation in conjunction with the adoption of a new IT system.	MOF, FRC, BOM, MCSD	MT

continued on next page

Continued

Recommendation	Agency	Timing[a]
Investor base		
3. Promote investor protection and broaden the investor base.		
(i) Continue to leverage the amended Investment Fund Law and existing tax incentives to further develop diverse investor profiles, including various types of investment funds, asset management firms, and insurance companies to expand the investment base for corporate bonds. This should involve revising regulatory hurdles that limit the range of instruments available for insurance company investments and updating pension fund regulations to allow pension funds to purchase corporate bonds and actively participate in the market.	MOF, FRC	MT
(ii) Address the lack of professional investors and foreign investors by simplifying procedural obligations and facilitating the entry of global custodians, thereby making the market more accessible to international participants.	MOF, FRC	MT
(iii) Clarify the regulatory definitions of "listing" and "registration" to eliminate confusion and revise restrictions that prevent mutual funds from accessing the over-the-counter bond market.	FRC	NT
(iv) Enhance financial literacy and retail investor education programs, with a focus on raising awareness and understanding of fixed-income instruments.	FRC, MASD	MT
(v) Introduce a regulatory framework for bondholder representatives or trustees to strengthen investor protection in the bond market.	FRC	MT
(vi) Develop the legal, operational, and risk management framework needed to implement omnibus accounts and connect the Mongolian Central Securities Depository to international central securities depositories such as Clearstream and Euroclear.	FRC, MCSD	MT
Issuer base		
4. Optimize government bond market development and enhance market participation.		
(i) Further develop the current system for issuing government bonds by instituting a primary dealer system that is adaptable to specific market conditions, adjusting maturity periods to better meet market demands, and establishing secondary market development incentives including market-making commitments from primary dealers, liquidity provision requirements, and performance-based allocation benefits that reward active secondary market participation and price discovery contributions.	MOF	MT
(ii) Focus on developing benchmark issues across the yield curve as the government bond market matures, ensuring sufficient liquidity in secondary markets and building fungible benchmark issues to enhance the market's utility as a pricing reference for corporate bonds.	MOF	NT

continued on next page

Continued

Recommendation	Agency	Timing[a]
(iii) Diversify the investor base for government bonds beyond commercial banks to include entities with varying risk appetites, such as mutual funds, pension funds, and insurance companies. Encourage securities companies to take an active role in developing repo markets and foster more active secondary trading to enhance overall market liquidity.	MOF, FRC	MT
(iv) Promote regulatory certainty and continued support of over-the-counter bond issuance to sustain access for issuers and reduce time-to-market, while maintaining investor protection standards.	FRC, MASD	MT
(v) Define "true sale" and "bankruptcy remoteness" under the Securities Market Law to provide a stable legal basis for securitization transactions in line with international practices.	FRC	MT
(vi) Support credit rating agency development through capacity building, technical assistance, and implementation of rating quality standards to ensure meaningful and trusted credit assessments in the bond market.	FRC	MT
Intermediation		
5. Consider introducing a primary dealer system for government bonds and raise securities company qualification requirements.		
(i) Introduce a primary dealer system aligned with local market conditions to establish a secondary market for government bonds, improving the efficiency of issuance and trading in the Mongolian government bond market while generating a much-needed benchmark interest rate for the financial market.	MOF, FRC	MT
(ii) Enhance intermediary credibility by introducing regulations that permit only investment banks with strong creditworthiness and technological capabilities to underwrite and broker corporate bonds. Reevaluate minimum capital requirements and accelerate the transition from paper-based processes through synchronized system enhancements across market participants.	FRC, MCSD	NT
(iii) Implement a tier-based licensing system for brokerage firms based on operational capabilities, capital adequacy, and technological readiness. Establish technical assistance programs for inactive firms and develop consolidation frameworks for firms unable to meet updated requirements.	FRC, MASD	NT
(iv) Explore options to broaden retail investor access to over-the-counter bond instruments, potentially through mutual funds, investment platforms, or fintech channels.	FRC, MASD	MT
(v) Establish a framework for reliable bond pricing using independent pricing services or credit rating agencies to strengthen transparency and investor confidence.	FRC, MASD, local credit rating agency	MT

BOM = Bank of Mongolia, FRC = Financial Regulatory Commission, IT = information technology, MASD = Mongolian Association of Securities Dealers, MCSD = Mongolian Central Securities Depository, MOF = Ministry of Finance, MSCC = Mongolian Securities Clearing Center, MSE = Mongolian Stock Exchange.

[a] NT = near term (within 1 year), MT = medium term (1–3 years).

Source: Authors.

INTRODUCTION 1

Background

A bond market is fundamentally important to economic development and the advancement of financial markets. Bonds serve as the primary source of long-term financing for countries, corporations, and financial institutions. For investors, bond markets serve the function of expanding the available fixed-income investment opportunities and developing the collective investment scheme market. They are also used as an instrument of monetary policy and as a key indicator for formulating and managing regulatory policies related to the financial markets. As a result, the establishment of efficient bond markets can play a role in increasing the resilience of the financial market to sudden changes and shocks.

Countries with underdeveloped bond markets may face constraints on large-scale, long-term financing by capital seekers (states, financial institutions, and corporations), which can slow economic development. Underdeveloped bond markets can also limit a country's ability to introduce various financial instruments utilizing bonds, leaving retail investors less able to build wealth and restricting the scope of investment opportunities for institutional investors. This ultimately hinders the development of the financial markets.

Driven by the introduction of various policies aimed at developing its bond market, Mongolia's local currency bond market (LCBM) is experiencing a resurgence. However, as this market continues to evolve and mature, there is a pressing need to improve the efficiency of the surrounding financial market infrastructures (FMIs) that support the bond market ecosystem.

Assessment Methodology

The Asian Development Bank (ADB) has developed *A Diagnostic Framework for the Local Currency Bond Market* (2024) to establish a systematic methodology for assessing the local LCBM of its developing member countries (DMCs). The diagnostic assessment aims to serve as a basis for ADB to provide operational support to the DMCs, helping them close the gaps identified by the assessment.

The framework reviews five dimensions that are crucial for the development of LCBMs: (i) legal and regulatory framework, (ii) FMIs, (iii) investor base, (iv) issuer base, and (v) intermediation. The first two dimensions analyze the institutional and systemic settings that facilitate the efficient and smooth operation of LCBMs. The last three dimensions examine key market participants by category.

The dimensions are composed of three to five subdimensions, resulting in a total of 18 subdimensions (Table 1). The assessment is conducted at the subdimension level by (i) describing the international standards and best practices; (ii) listing key questions for examining the country's status; and (iii) providing four benchmarks for assessment: fully implemented, broadly implemented, partially implemented, and not implemented.

Table 1: Dimensions of a Diagnostic Framework for the Local Currency Bond Market

Dimension (5)	Subdimension (18)
1. Legal and regulatory framework	1.1. Long-term development plan for capital market
	1.2. Bond market: Overall
	1.3. Primary bond market
	1.4. Secondary bond market
	1.5. Green, social, and sustainability bonds
2. Financial market infrastructures	2.1. Payment system
	2.2. Central securities depository/securities settlement system
	2.3. Central counterparty
3. Investor base	3.1. Institutional investor base
	3.2. Retail investor base
	3.3. Foreign investor base
	3.4. Investor protection
4. Issuer base	4.1. Potential issuers
	4.2. Securitization
	4.3. Credit rating agencies
5. Intermediation	5.1. Intermediaries: Brokers and dealers
	5.2. Trading platforms
	5.3. Transparency of trading and pricing

Source: ADB consultant.

Data for quantitative indicators were collected from relevant public resources first and then from stakeholders if the information was unavailable. Information for qualitative indicators was collected from the literature review, stakeholders' feedback on questionnaires, and stakeholder interviews. Based on the data and information gathered, the key issues at the subdimension level were identified and then prioritized at the dimension level. Recommendations to close the identified gaps were drawn from international standards and best practices with adaptations to the country context.

By synthesizing benchmark results of subdimensions, each dimension is rated at one of these four stages:

- Stage 1 (Initial): No relevant policies are in place, or no functions exist.
- Stage 2 (Development): The relevant policies or measures are functioning to a certain extent, but there are constraints on their practical implementation.
- Stage 3 (Growth): The policies or measures are functioning but need further improvement.
- Stage 4 (Mature): The policies or measures are effectively functioning, and the market is active.

Based on the results of this diagnostic assessment, a diagram summarizes the current stages of the five dimensions in the country under assessment, with the outermost pentagon at Stage 4 (Mature) for all dimensions (Figure 1). This comparison allows for immediate identification of areas for improvement, which can then be used to propose strategies and road maps to close the gaps. An expanded diagram illustrates the expected outcome once the country completes the implementation of the near-term (within 1 year) and medium-term (1–3 years) recommendations.

Figure 1: Summary of Assessment Results (Conceptual)

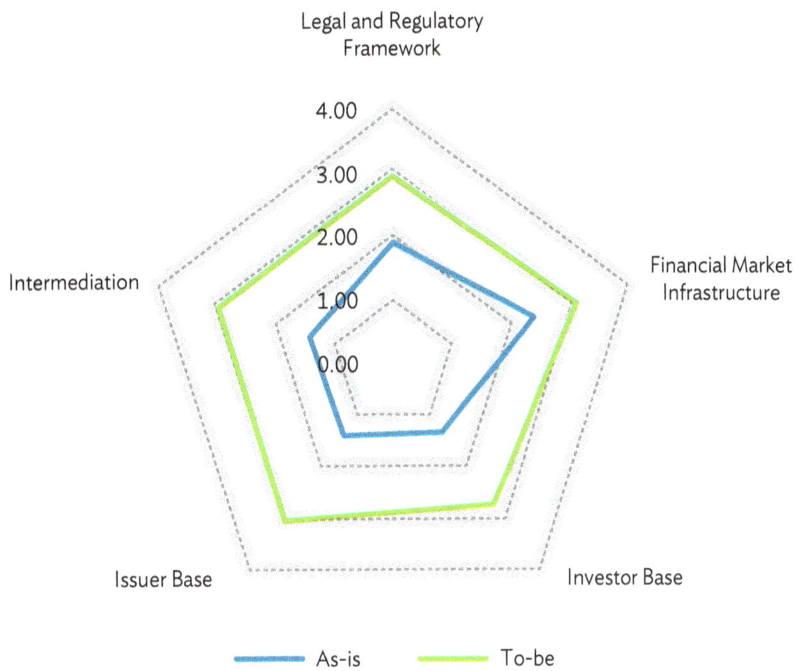

Note: Stage 1 (Initial) – Stage 2 (Development) – Stage 3 (Growth) – Stage 4 (Mature).

Source: ADB consultant.

ASSESSMENT OF LOCAL CURRENCY BOND MARKET IN MONGOLIA

2

Legal and Regulatory Framework

Long-Term Development Plan for Capital Market

Since Mongolia transitioned to a market-driven economy in 1990, its financial market and regulatory framework have evolved significantly. The Mongolian Stock Exchange (MSE), established in 1991, has played a pivotal role in privatizing state-owned entities, transferring ownership of 475 companies to approximately 1.2 million citizens.

The Securities Market Law was first introduced in 1994, creating the now-dissolved Securities Committee of the Bank of Mongolia (BOM) to regulate the capital market. Secondary market trading for securities commenced in 1995, and the first government bonds were traded in 1996, while the first corporate bond was issued in 2001.

During the early 2010s, Mongolia attracted increased interest in its mining sector from foreign investors. Significant revisions and additions have been made to capital market regulations since 2013 to attract more foreign investors into the domestic market and to stay current with global financial and capital markets.

The Securities Market Law (amended on 24 May 2013, effective 1 January 2014) regulates the monitoring of activities by participants in the securities market and the protection of investors' rights and interests. The scope of the law encompasses securities issues, including corporate debt securities, through public offers, trading, and the registration of securities; clearing, settlement, and deposit of securities; and other regulated activities in the securities market.

The Financial Regulatory Commission (FRC), established in 2006, oversees the securities market, among other finance sectors. Its mandate includes ensuring market stability, developing regulations, and supervising market participants. The Ministry of Finance (MOF), which is responsible for budget policies and government bond issuance, plays a crucial role in the development of Mongolia's capital market. The MOF is responsible for government bond issuance both internationally and domestically and serves as an issuer and regulator of local currency government bonds in the domestic market under the Debt Management Law (enacted on 18 February 2015). In addition, the MOF owns and has the power to appoint all the directors of many of the main capital market regulating entities (e.g., the MSE, the Mongolian Central Securities Depository [MCSD], and the Mongolian Securities Clearing House [MSCH]). Therefore it plays an important role in the development of the domestic capital market.

Legislators and regulators in Mongolia are implementing various long-term programs to help develop the Mongolian bond market and the capital market as a whole. As part of the tax policy reform introduced in 2019, corporate and personal income taxes on interest income from publicly offered corporate debt instruments were lowered from 10% to 5% starting in January 2020.

In addition, the government has revised legislation related to the capital market to create a legal environment that promotes competition and accessibility in the finance sector, increasing product offerings, and streamlining regulations.

The adoption of amendments to the Securities Market Law on 16 May 2024 represents a significant milestone in Mongolia's capital market development strategy. These amendments strategically differentiate between exchange and over-the-counter (OTC) markets, support collective investment schemes, and simplify the process of issuing securities through underwriting companies. The revised law aims to lower issuance costs and increase quality product offerings in the market.

It is noteworthy that the amendments include several measures related to risk management in the securities market. To manage the principal risk of the securities market, an upgrade of the delivery versus payment (DVP) system was implemented and regulations were introduced to implement comprehensive clearing risk management mechanisms of the central counterparty (CCP) to manage the credit risk of market participants. These include the regulation of qualification and necessary conditions for clearing members and the establishment of a clearing fund (referred to as the Settlement Guarantee Fund).

The FRC's rights have been expanded to accommodate technological progress and facilitate regulatory sandbox environments, positioning Mongolia to adapt more quickly to financial technology innovations. Furthermore, the amendments clarify the rights, obligations, and responsibilities of custodian banks, improve information transparency and corporate governance of publicly listed companies, protect minority shareholders' interests, and enhance company disclosure requirements.

A significant advancement in the regulatory architecture is the delegation of certain FRC responsibilities to self-regulatory organizations (SROs). This approach, aligned with international best practices, enhances regulatory expertise and enforcement efficiency by leveraging industry-specific knowledge and resources. SROs can develop more tailored and practical rules that reflect current market conditions, reducing overall regulatory compliance costs and administrative burdens for market participants. This flexibility enables market participants to develop their operations and adopt new practices in a timely manner, aligning with Mongolia's civil code-based legal system.

Overall Bond Market

Mongolia's bond market is regulated separately for government bonds and corporate bonds. Government bonds are regulated by the Debt Management Law (enacted on 18 February 2015) and the Government Resolution Regarding the Regulation of Primary and Secondary Market Operations of Domestic Government Securities (No. 77, 20 February 2019), which governs only government bond issuance procedures and government debt ceilings.

Local currency government bond issuance was halted indefinitely in October 2017 under the Extended Fund Facility (EFF) program of the International Monetary Fund (IMF). The EFF, which was approved on 24 May 2017 and concluded on 31 October 2018, was part of a larger $5.5 billion multidonor financing package supporting Mongolia's Economic Recovery Plan. The program aimed to support Mongolia's economic reform initiatives, including increasing fiscal discipline, rehabilitating the finance sector, promoting investment and employment, and strengthening the social safety net. During this period, the suspension of government bond issuance was part of the broader fiscal consolidation measures required under the program.

Following the successful completion of the IMF program and the subsequent economic recovery, the MOF restarted issuance of government domestic securities on 16 April 2025, in line with Goal 4 of the Government's Medium-Term Debt Management Strategy 2023–2025. This restart aims to support the domestic government bond market and establish a benchmark interest rate for local currency bonds in the financial market. Government bonds represent the least risky and most liquid financial instruments for investors, with interest income exempt from income tax. Additionally, under the Law on Procurement of Goods, Works, and Services with State and Local Property, businesses can now use Mongolian government securities as tender guarantees for performance and advance payments. The resumption of regular government bond issuance is crucial for developing the domestic debt market, providing a reliable way to finance budget deficits and establishing a risk-free yield curve that serves as a benchmark for the broader capital market.

The corporate bond market is based on the Company Law and the Securities Market Law. The Company Law stipulates the establishment, registration, and reorganization of a company; its shareholding and organizational structure; rights and obligations; and other related matters. The Securities Market Law covers securities issues, including corporate debt securities, through public offers, trading, and the registration of securities; as well as clearing, settlement, and deposit of securities; and other regulated activities in the securities market. The law provides general regulation of the issuance and trading of asset-backed securities. Detailed regulation of asset-backed securities is provided through the Asset-Backed Securities Market Law, enacted on 23 April 2010 and effective as of 1 January 2011.

Although a bond is defined in the Securities Market Law as a type of securities, it is termed a "debt instrument," and there is no mention of the term "bond" in the law. Therefore, even though participants in the Mongolian capital market understand the term "bond," the legal terminology for bond is "debt instrument." There are no terms such as short-term notes, commercial paper, or short-term bills in the capital market related regulations. In addition, debt instruments are treated as a type of securities, and no special distinction is made in the law except when additional requirements are enforced when issuing them. Therefore, in addition to shares, all necessary documentation and procedures required with for securities are also applied equally to publicly issued debt instruments. Privately placed corporate debt instruments are outside the scope of the Securities Market Law and were not regulated by the FRC. This resulted in the emergence of an unregulated, privately placed corporate debt instruments market, which was dominated by the larger securities brokerage firms.

To address these issues, the FRC introduced the Regulation on Debt Instrument Registration (June 2021), which, for the first time, introduced the term "bond" in securities market regulations and established differentiated requirements for issuing bonds compared to equity securities. This regulatory framework provided clarity and structure specifically tailored to bond markets, creating a foundation for more organized bond issuance and trading activities.

Additionally, the FRC introduced the Regulation on Operation of the OTC Market (December 2020), which established a regulatory framework for the OTC market.[1] The introduction of the OTC regulatory framework allowed the regulation of previously unregulated privately placed corporate bonds. It also allowed companies to issue bonds through a more flexible and streamlined process. Under this regulation, the Mongolian Association of Securities Dealers (MASD), an SRO, manages the daily operations of the OTC market.

The amended Securities Market Law addresses several critical aspects of bond market regulation. The law now provides a clearer definition of bonds as debt instruments and establishes a more flexible framework for bond issuance, trading, and settlement.

While the law establishes general principles, it strategically leaves detailed regulatory aspects to the FRC, allowing for more responsive adaptation to market developments. This approach provides regulatory flexibility that aligns with international best practices in jurisdictions with similar civil code traditions.

However, further development is needed in areas concerning bondholders' representation. International examples from civil law jurisdictions such as France, Germany, and the Republic of Korea demonstrate the effectiveness of clear legal frameworks for bondholders' representatives or trustees. These jurisdictions have established specific fiduciary duties for representatives while maintaining regulatory flexibility. For instance, the German Debt Securities Act (Schuldverschreibungsgesetz) provides a comprehensive framework for bondholders' meetings and their representatives, while allowing market participants flexibility in its implementation.

Primary Bond Market

Bond Issuance Process

The Securities Market Law outlines the procedures for municipal and corporate bond issuances through public offers, trading, and the registration of securities; clearing, settlement, and deposit of securities; and other regulated activities. The Regulation on Debt Instrument Registration defines the procedures for publicly issuing municipal and corporate bonds, while the Regulation on Operation of the OTC Market regulates private placements of municipal and corporate bonds.

The amendments to the Securities Market Law have harmonized the legal framework with the FRC's updated regulations for bond registration, effectively addressing the previous discrepancies between the law and regulatory practices. The streamlined approach for issuing debt securities in the primary market is now aligned with the regulatory framework.

The revised law introduces a simplified process for public offerings through underwriting companies while maintaining necessary investor protections. This balanced approach follows international best practices observed in markets such as the Republic of Korea and Malaysia, where streamlined issuance procedures are combined with robust disclosure requirements.

1 "Over the counter market" is translated as "non-exchange market" in the Mongolian language.

Government Bond Issuance Process

Government bonds are regulated under the Debt Management Law and the Regulation on Issuance and Trading of Primary and Secondary Market Government Securities, with the MOF responsible for formulating regulations governing the primary and secondary markets for government securities as per Article 26 of the Debt Management Law.

Prior to the suspension of government bond issuance in 2017, local currency government bonds were issued through two separate venues: on the exchange market for retail investors and OTC market through BOM systems for wholesale investors such as banks. Exchange market issuances were conducted at the MSE for what was termed the "retail government bond market," accessible to individuals and banks operating through brokers. OTC market issuances were organized through the BOM-operated interbank OTC market, known as the "wholesale government bond market," exclusively accessible to local banks.

Local currency government bond issuance resumed in April 2025 with a streamlined, unified system that replaced the previous dual-venue structure. The new framework operates through the MSE's electronic platform (bond.mse.mn), where all investors—retail, institutional, and banks—participate through licensed brokerage firms.

The government conducts biweekly auctions every other Wednesday from 10:00 a.m. to 11:00 a.m., offering bonds across three maturity categories: short-term (up to 1 year), medium-term (1–5 years), and long-term (over 5 years). Short-term bonds are issued as discount instruments, while longer maturities feature fixed coupons. Investors can submit two types of bids: competitive bids (specifying both yield and quantity) or noncompetitive bids (quantity only). To promote market development, allocations to a single investor are capped at 25% of each issuance.

Secondary Bond Market

The Securities Market Law and the FRC Regulation on Debt Instrument Registration provide the legal basis for the secondary market for publicly issued bonds. Once the primary market issuance is concluded, the issuer must submit a report on the successful primary market issuance to the FRC to obtain approval to commence secondary market trading. The Securities Market Law and the FRC Regulation primarily outline the information disclosure requirements, while the exchanges set the trading rules. The Mongolian Securities Clearing Center (MSCC) handles the clearing and settlement of publicly offered corporate debt securities at the MSE.

The amended Securities Market Law addresses inefficiencies in clearing and settlement processes through comprehensive updates to the regulatory framework governing FMIs. The law now provides clearer guidance on the roles and responsibilities of market participants, particularly in relation to clearing and settlement functions.

The implementation of a DVP mechanism, supported by the legal framework, significantly reduces settlement risk and aligns with international standards. Additionally, the creation of a settlement guarantee fund enhances market stability and investor confidence.

Securities trading on both the exchanges and the OTC market are conducted electronically. Settlement is conducted at T+2 at the MSE, while the OTC market has the option to settle at T+0 or T+1 on a DVP basis.

Currently, there is no secondary market for local currency government bonds.

Green, Social, and Sustainability Bonds

As a result of the approval of Mongolia's Green Taxonomy by the Financial Stability Board of the Parliament in 2019, Mongolia became one of the first countries in the world to approve a green taxonomy.[2] Following this, the FRC updated its Regulation on Debt Instrument Registration in 2021 to align with the internationally recognized Green Bond Principles.[3] This regulatory update paved the way for the issuance of Green, Social, and Sustainability (GSS) bonds in Mongolia.

The issuance process for GSS bonds follows a rigorous framework, including the option to add an independent external review to assess the alignment of the proposed bond with the Green Taxonomy and the Green Bond Principles. Additionally, issuers must disclose detailed information about the use of proceeds, project selection criteria, and management of proceeds, which is subject to review by the FRC.

After issuance, GSS bond issuers are required to provide regular updates on the allocation of proceeds and the environmental or social impact achieved through the funded projects. This disclosure system ensures transparency and accountability, enabling investors to monitor the alignment of their investments with the stated objectives of the GSS bonds. The FRC closely monitors these disclosures to maintain market integrity and investor confidence.

Following the groundwork laid by the Green Taxonomy and the 2021 Regulation on Debt Instrument Registration, Khan Bank, Mongolia's largest commercial bank, successfully issued the country's first GSS Bond to international investors such as the International Finance Corporation, among others, in March 2023.[4] Building on this success, Khan Bank issued its first green bond listed on the MSE in October 2024 under the first green thematic bond program on the exchange. This landmark issuance included a $25 million tranche fully subscribed by strategic international investors such as ADB and the European Bank for Reconstruction and Development, and an additional MNT17 billion (approximately $5 million) tranche offered to local retail investors.[5] While this pioneering issuance paves the way for a more robust green bond market in Mongolia, further issuances are needed to fully establish this segment of the capital market.

2 World Bank. 2020. *Developing a National Green Taxonomy: A World Bank Guide*. July.

3 In June 2021, the Financial Regulatory Commission approved green bond regulations as part of the Company Debt Instrument Registration Regulation, developed with assistance from the International Finance Corporation to align with the internationally recognized Green Bond Principles. See, T. Baljma. 2021. A new regulation on 'Green Bond' approved to boost green finance in Mongolia. Montsame. 6 June.

4 IFC. 2023. IFC Invests in Mongolia's First Ever Green Bond in a Bid to Spur Climate-Smart Investments. Press release. 17 March.

5 ADB. 2024. ADB Invests $12.5 Million in Khan Bank's Milestone Green Bonds, a First in Mongolia. Press release. 15 October.

Assessment and Recommendations: Legal and Regulatory Framework

Long-term development plan for capital market. With the recent amendments to the Securities Market Law enacted on 16 May 2024, significant progress has been made in addressing many regulatory issues in Mongolia's capital market. The amendments introduce a more flexible regulatory approach that allows the FRC to adopt regulations according to market developments. The successful resumption of local currency government bond issuance in April 2025 represents a major milestone in addressing the long-standing absence of a government bond yield curve, which had previously hampered the development of the Mongolian bond market.

The reestablishment of regular government bond issuance creates opportunities for broader capital market development. As the government bond market matures and trading volumes increase, it will serve as the foundation for developing more sophisticated financial instruments, including securities lending and borrowing (SLB) and repo markets. The current biweekly issuance schedule provides a steady flow of instruments across different maturities, which should gradually establish a reliable yield curve that benefits the entire bond market.

Furthermore, the development of a comprehensive bond custodian regime would be beneficial, drawing on successful models from comparable markets in Asia. This would help facilitate cross-border investment flows and align Mongolia's bond market infrastructure with international best practices, building upon the clarified rights and responsibilities of custodian banks in the recently amended Securities Market Law.

Overall bond market. While the amended Securities Market Law provides a more flexible regulatory framework, it could be further enhanced by drawing on specific examples from civil law jurisdictions such as France, Germany, and the Republic of Korea regarding bond default events and bondholders' representation. Although there have been no instances of bond default in the local market, the absence of explicit provisions for handling bond default and cross-default scenarios poses a potential risk. In addition, the existing laws in Mongolia do not recognize the concept of a bondholders' representative or bond trustee. As a result, market practice has led to bond underwriters assuming the role of bondholders' representatives under each bond's underwriting contract. This practice creates a potential conflict of interest, however. The underwriter's primary commitment is toward the issuer for bond sales facilitation, while the role of a bondholders' representative or trustee is inherently aligned with safeguarding bondholders' interests.

Primary bond market. The amendment of the Securities Market resolved previous discrepancies by establishing consistency with the FRC regulations for bond registration. The law now provides a general framework that gives the FRC flexibility to adapt detailed regulations as the market develops. This approach is appropriate for Mongolia's civil code legal system and helps ensure that the regulatory framework can evolve with market needs.

Secondary bond market. The amendments to the Securities Market Law address many of the inefficiencies in the clearing and settlement processes through updates on the DVP mechanism and regulations for managing insolvency risk. The establishment of a settlement guarantee fund and clearing members framework will help enhance market stability. However, continued refinement of the operational frameworks of a Central Securities Depository (CSD) or a Securities Settlement System (SSS) will be necessary to fully implement these legal provisions and accommodate increasing market activity.

GSS bonds. The deployment of sustainability-linked bonds offers a strategic method to mitigate risks such as greenwashing, whereby issuers may falsely claim environmental friendliness despite insufficient actual impact. By linking interest rates to the issuer's performance on GSS criteria, these bonds provide verifiable accountability. Developing a framework for sustainability-linked bonds necessitates establishing an infrastructure capable of selecting essential performance indicators and accurately measuring sustainability targets.

However, the current regulatory framework, while comprehensive, involves process-heavy requirements that limit accessibility primarily to large financial institutions with sufficient resources to navigate the complex compliance procedures. To broaden market participation and enhance the GSS bond framework, streamlining the current regulatory processes without compromising the integrity of green finance principles should be considered. This could include developing simplified procedures for smaller issuers or creating tiered requirements based on issuer size and complexity.

Furthermore, formulating a reasoned approach for integrating performance-based interest rate mechanisms is essential for the effective implementation of sustainability-linked bonds. However, identifying specific regulatory deficiencies is premature, given the limited number of GSS bond issuances to date. As market activity increases and more diverse issuers participate in this segment, practical experience will provide valuable insights into potential regulatory refinements needed to balance market accessibility with green finance principles. Therefore, a comprehensive review of the current GSS bond regulatory framework should be conducted once sufficient market data becomes available, after reaching a critical mass of issuances that would allow for meaningful assessment of regulatory effectiveness and market development needs.

Self-regulatory organizations and delegated functions. While the amended Securities Market Law delegates certain FRC responsibilities to SROs, the governance framework for these delegated functions requires further clarification. MASD, which manages the OTC market as an SRO, plays a crucial role in market operations. To ensure regulatory consistency and accountability, Mongolia needs clearer guidelines on the scope of delegated powers, reporting requirements, oversight mechanisms, and procedures for ensuring that the SRO regulatory activities align with the FRC overall policy objectives. Drawing on international best practices from jurisdictions with mature SRO frameworks, Mongolia should establish clear boundaries between SRO functions and direct regulatory oversight, while maintaining the flexibility that makes the SRO model attractive for market development. Additionally, the framework should address potential conflicts of interest, establish clear disciplinary procedures, and ensure adequate resources and expertise within SROs to effectively carry out their delegated responsibilities.

Legal terminology harmonization. The current legal framework creates potential confusion by using different terminology for the same financial instruments. While the Securities Market Law uses the term "debt instrument," market participants and the FRC regulations have adopted the more internationally recognized term "bond." This inconsistency in terminology across various legal documents and regulations creates unnecessary complexity for both domestic and international investors. Harmonizing the terminology to consistently use "bond" throughout all relevant laws and regulations would align Mongolia's legal framework with international market conventions, reduce potential misunderstandings, and enhance the market's accessibility to foreign investors who are accustomed to standard global terminology.

Table 2: Summary of Recommendations—Legal and Regulatory Framework

Recommendation	Agency	Timing[a]
Further enhance the legal and regulatory framework to bolster mechanisms protecting investors, especially in default situations, and to streamline settlement processes and custody while maintaining regulatory flexibility.		
(i) Building on the amended Securities Market Law, develop FRC regulations to provide more detailed provisions addressing bond defaults and cross-default situations, drawing on international examples from civil law jurisdictions such as France, Germany, and the Republic of Korea.	FRC	MT
(ii) Implement a regulatory framework to oversee the appointment and functioning of bondholders' representatives or trustees, particularly in bond default and cross-default scenarios, ensuring their actions align with the best interests of bondholders and international best practices. Establish clear separation between bond underwriters and bondholders' representatives or trustees to prevent conflicts of interest, with this separation enforced through regulatory guidelines that ensure fiduciary duties toward bondholders are not compromised.	FRC	MT
(iii) Continue refining the operational frameworks of Financial Market Infrastructures to fully implement the provisions of the amended Securities Market Law, particularly those related to clearing, settlement, and custody services.	MOF, FRC, MCSD	NT
(iv) Develop a comprehensive bond custodian regime aligned with the amended Securities Market Law that establishes clear custody arrangements to facilitate cross-border investment flows. This regime must simultaneously support the creation of a government bond yield curve and enable the development of a secondary market and key instruments, such as securities lending and repo.	MOF, FRC, MCSD	MT
(v) Review the regulatory framework for the issuance of green, social, and sustainability bonds once sufficient market data is available to assess its effectiveness.	FRC	MT
(vi) Clarify and strengthen the governance and oversight framework for self-regulatory organizations to ensure consistency in delegated regulatory functions and accountability aligned with international best practices.	FRC, MASD	NT
(vii) Harmonize terminology in relevant laws and regulations to standardize the use of "bond" across legal documents and align with international market conventions and investor expectations.	MOF, FRC	NT

FRC = Financial Regulatory Committee, MASD = Mongolian Association of Securities Dealers, MCSD = Mongolian Central Securities Depository, MOF = Ministry of Finance.

[a] NT = near term (within 1 year), MT = medium term (1–3 years).

Source: Authors.

Financial Market Infrastructures

The responsibilities for Mongolia's financial market infrastructures (FMIs) are divided as follows: the Central Bank manages the payment systems; the MCSD manages the CSD and SSS; and the MSCC is responsible for the Central Counterparty.

The institutional framework and operational procedures of these FMIs are primarily regulated by the Securities Market Law and the Central Bank Law. The Securities Market Law governs the exchange, depository, and post-trade systems, encompassing all aspects of securities trading, clearing, and settlement. The Central Bank Law outlines the functions of the BOM, including its role as a financial intermediary for the government, its supervisory authority over commercial banks, and its management of the national payment system.

Authorities for Financial Market Infrastructures

The Principles for Financial Market Infrastructures (PFMI) emphasize the importance of strong institutional support for FMIs to ensure their efficiency and stability. Fortunately, Mongolia has a well-established framework to address this need. Several key institutions play a vital role in promoting financial stability and efficiency, including the MOF, the FRC, and the BOM. These entities collaborate through a consultative body known as the Financial Market Stability Council. The council's primary objective is to safeguard financial stability by proactively identifying and managing potential risks within the existing legal and regulatory framework. To achieve this, the council conducts research and makes recommendations to address current challenges and promote a sound and resilient financial market in Mongolia.

Payment System

The real-time gross settlement system, managed by the BOM, supports the Mongolian capital market's transactions. The MCSD, a state-owned entity under MOF oversight, maintains a correspondent account at the BOM, facilitating a robust DVP service that ensures synchronized settlements of securities and cash.

Central Securities Depository/Securities Settlement System

The MCSD holds a monopoly as Mongolia's sole CSD and administers the SSS. Governed by the FRC under special licenses, the MCSD performs registration and depository functions for government and corporate bonds across primary and secondary markets.

The settlement process within the MCSD executes securities settlements on a gross basis and cash settlements on a net basis, culminating in a combined DVP execution at noon on the T+2 settlement date.

Central Counterparty

The Mongolian Securities Clearing House & Central Depository was reorganized in 2016, leading to the creation of the MCSD for securities registration and safekeeping and the MSCC for clearing and settlement. Current legislation does not explicitly define the role or risk management obligations of a central counterparty (CCP).

The current clearing system used by the MSCC is the E-Clear system, introduced in 2007 by the Mongolian Securities Clearing House & Central Depository, the predecessor of the MSCC.[6] Given that the current E-Clear system was introduced prior to the implementation of the PFMI in 2012, there are concerns regarding its capability to adhere to PFMI risk management principles.

Assessment and Recommendations: Financial Market Infrastructures

Authorities for FMIs. To enhance the efficiency of the Mongolian FMI, it is recommended to establish a dedicated committee, tentatively named the "Capital Market Efficiency Committee." This committee, comprising experts from Mongolian capital market policy-making bodies and academia, would fulfill the following key functions:

(i) Establish and implement a policy for the short-term migration to DEPO/X or other new systems.[7]

(ii) Establish a mid- to long-term strategy for enhanced post-trade efficiency in the capital market. This strategy should be based on clearly defined roles and responsibilities for each FMI and include detailed implementation plans, encompassing resource allocation (human resources, budget, etc.).

Financial market stability council coordination. While the Financial Market Stability Council provides a valuable framework for interagency coordination, its role in FMI modernization efforts requires strengthening to ensure effective national coordination. The current fragmented approach to FMI development, exemplified by separate system procurement and implementation processes across different institutions, highlights the need for enhanced coordination mechanisms. Strengthening the Financial Market Stability Council's coordination function would help align FMI modernization efforts, ensure regulatory coherence across different supervisory bodies, and prevent duplication of resources.

Payment system. The BOM embarked on the Payment System Modernization Project in 2013. In May 2023, the payment functionalities of DEPO/X, utilized by the BOM, were successfully launched. Through this project, the BOM has not only expanded the range of available functions, but has also upgraded the existing real-time gross settlement system. The CSD functionalities to be used by MCSD will go live upon completion of necessary procedures, such as DEPO/X functionality tests. The BOM will continue to support this endeavor.

---

[6] The E-Clear IT system was developed by ECM LLC, a local software company, for securities settlement and deposit functions in 2007.

[7] DEPO/X is an IT system developed as a CSD solution by a Swedish IT company called CMA.

CSD and SSS. The MCSD, which operates the SSS as the country's central depository, faces the following challenges:

(i) The MCSD's IT system, established 18 years ago, underpins the SSS and other critical infrastructures. However, its outdated technology raises concerns about its ability to support the introduction of new financial products and services. The BOM acquired a new IT system, DEPO/X, as part of its own infrastructure modernization efforts, which offers various features and functionalities that could potentially be used by MCSD. However, the MCSD was not involved in the procurement and implementation process of this system. A comprehensive review is needed to determine the optimal path forward: either migrating to the BOM's DEPO/X system or supporting the MCSD in developing/procuring its own system. This decision should prioritize long-term operational efficiency and customization needs, allowing the MCSD to better align system capabilities with its specific operational requirements and maintain appropriate control over future system enhancements and modifications.

(ii) The Mongolian securities market currently claims to utilize DVP Model 2. However, a close examination of settlement practices against the established characteristics of DVP Model 2, as outlined in the PFMI, reveals discrepancies. In simple terms, the Mongolian securities market is not fully realizing the benefits of DVP Model 2. A review and potential adjustments are necessary to achieve true DVP Model 2 implementation.[8]

(iii) The Mongolian securities market presents a timely opportunity to accelerate development through the introduction of innovative financial instruments. Market participants have expressed strong interest in using securities lending and borrowing and repurchase agreements (repos), but their implementation should be carefully coordinated with IT system modernization efforts to ensure efficient integration. The introduction of these mechanisms should be planned in conjunction with the broader FMI development strategy to maximize operational synergies and minimize implementation costs.

CCP. The transformation of the MSCC into a CCP aligned with international best practices requires several crucial modifications. These are the most pressing areas for improvement:

(i) The primary step toward establishing the MSCC as a CCP with international consistency is to develop a robust legal framework aligned with PFMI requirements. This framework should incorporate key principles such as "open offer" and "novation," as outlined in the PFMI, to solidify the MSCC's position and legal authority as a CCP.

(ii) Upgrading the MSCC's IT infrastructure is another critical step. The current 18-year-old E-Clear system is unable to fully support modern risk management practices. While the newly acquired DEPO/X offers DVP functionalities, it lacks a clearing function. Therefore, the MSCC should prioritize the acquisition of a new IT system specifically designed to handle clearing activities and integrate seamlessly with risk management tools.

(iii) In conjunction with the introduction of a new IT system, the MSCC must upgrade its current risk management practices to meet international standards. This includes reviewing clearing membership criteria, the adequacy of the settlement guarantee fund, and the efficiency of the margin system. A detailed discussion of these areas is contained in a separate Working Paper (available upon request).[9]

---

8 DVP model and recommendations for the Mongolian capital market are detailed in the Working Paper for Mongolia, Project Number: 54122-001. Refer to Chapter III of the Working Paper.

9 Refer to Working Paper for Mongolia, Project Number: 54122-001.

Table 3: Summary of Recommendations—Financial Market Infrastructure

Recommendation	Agency	Timing[a]
Develop a unified approach for the advancement and implementation of financial market infrastructure systems to address coordination gaps and enhance operational effectiveness.		
(i) Establish a specialized organization, tentatively named the "Capital Market Efficiency Committee," to plan and implement advancements in efficiency for post-trade settlement and clearing activities.	MOF, FRC, BOM	NT
(ii) Strengthen the coordination function of the Financial Market Stability Council to align national financial market infrastructure modernization efforts and ensure regulatory coherence across financial market infrastructures and supervisory bodies.	MOF, FRC, BOM	MT
(iii) Bolster capital market infrastructure by supporting the MCSD to either migrate to the BOM's DEPO/X system or develop/procure its own IT system to replace the outdated central securities depository/securities settlement system infrastructure, prioritizing the option that best serves long-term operational efficiency and customization needs.	MOF, FRC, BOM, MCSD, MSCC	MT
(iv) Review the introduction of a central counterparty system to efficiently manage credit risk in the capital markets, including the adoption of legal frameworks and risk management systems aligned with the Principles for Financial Market Infrastructures.	MOF, FRC, MSCC	MT
(v) Validate the effectiveness of the current DVP model and implement a DVP framework aligned with the Principles for Financial Market Infrastructures to efficiently manage principal risk in the capital market.	MOF, FRC, MCSD, MSCC	NT
(vi) Foster qualitative growth in Mongolia's capital markets by reviewing the introduction of liquidity provision mechanisms such as securities lending and borrowing and tri-party repo, ensuring efficient implementation in conjunction with the adoption of a new IT system.	MOF, FRC, BOM, MCSD	MT

DVP = delivery versus payment, FRC = Financial Regulatory Commission, MCSD = Mongolian Central Securities Depository, MOF = Ministry of Finance, MSCC = Mongolian Securities Clearing Center, MSE = Mongolian Stock Exchange.

[a] NT = near term (within 1 year), MT = medium term (1–3 years).

Source: Authors.

Investor Base

Institutional Investor Base

The institutional investor landscape in Mongolia is nascent. Pension funds are integrated into the national budget, while private pension schemes are still in their infancy. Regulatory constraints on the insurance sector limit its growth as a source of institutional investment. The limitations on post-trade services supporting cross-border bond trades also mean that foreign investment (especially in sovereign debt) is expected to remain limited in the near term.

The insurance sector, which focuses on automotive insurance, with minimal activity in life insurance, and lacks substantial long-term reserves, limiting its capacity to invest significantly in the bond market. The sector's growth is further hindered by stringent investment regulations that restrict the range of instruments available for insurance company investments, reducing overall market participation in fixed-income securities.

However, there has been a recent uptick in collective investment schemes (such as mutual funds), expanding the institutional investor base. Under the amended Investment Fund Law, various types of investment funds are now permitted to operate more actively. In particular, private equity funds can be established on both a contractual basis and as legal entities, providing more flexibility and opportunities for institutional investors. Tax incentives are already in place that offer tax exemptions for income generated from investment fund operations, further enhancing the attractiveness of these vehicles. Nonetheless, the long-term viability of these funds is often questioned by the public due to issues of mismanagement and the challenges of capital deployment caused by liquidity constraints in the capital markets. Consequently, most publicly traded mutual funds currently trade below their net asset value, reflecting investors' concerns regarding the funds' performance and underlying asset valuations.

Retail Investor Base

In the case of corporate bonds, the investor pool is predominantly comprised of high-net-worth individuals, with foreign investors discouraged by onerous paperwork requirements. Meanwhile, retail investors can only buy and sell publicly issued corporate bonds traded on the MSE.

The OTC market, established under the FRC Regulation on Operation of the OTC Market in September 2021, is accessible only to institutional investors, professional investors, and high-net-worth individuals. The regulation introduced requirements for net-worth size and investment experience for a high-net-worth individual to be considered a professional investor, thereby developing a professional investor market segment.

Foreign Investor Base

Foreign investment in Mongolia's local currency bond market (LCBM) is rare despite the country's high nominal interest rates due to currency depreciation risks. Procedural hurdles and complex documentation requirements for foreign investors to open brokerage accounts also pose significant barriers. The absence of global custodians further complicates Mongolia's positioning as an attractive destination for foreign investment, with most foreign investors engaging in the market through US dollar-denominated sovereign and corporate bonds issued internationally.

Investor Protection

Investor protection measures in Mongolia are governed by the Securities Market Law and supplementary regulations, encompassing mandatory information disclosure, dispute resolution mechanisms for insider trading, and market manipulation oversight. The Bankruptcy Law addresses insolvency issues and procedures applicable to Mongolian enterprises and cooperatives.

In addition, as part of its duties, the MASD promotes ethical business practices and investor protection, enforcing disciplinary actions against noncompliant member firms and individuals.

Regarding bond default provisions, Mongolia's Civil Code and Bankruptcy Law clearly define defaulting payment obligations. The Securities Market Law does not provide another definition of defaulting payment obligations, as these are adequately covered in the existing legal framework. However, there could be benefits to considering the role of bondholders' representatives or trustees to enhance investor protection in the specific context of bond markets.

Assessment and Recommendations: Investor Base

Institutional investor base. Continue to develop a diverse investor base, leveraging the amended Investment Fund Law to encourage more active participation by various investment funds, including private equity funds that can now be established with greater flexibility. The existing tax incentives for investment fund operations should be more widely promoted to increase awareness and participation. Further broadening of the investor base will also help broaden the investment base for future reintroduction of government bonds.

Current regulatory limitations hinder the expansion of the institutional investor base in the OTC bond market. For example, mutual funds are restricted by FRC regulations to investing only in listed securities, thereby excluding them from the OTC market due to a regulatory distinction between "listing" and "registration." The FRC needs to clarify these terms, as they are represented by the same word in Mongolian, creating confusion because the OTC market involves only registered instruments. Additionally, conservative reserve management policies for insurance companies and pension funds limit institutional participation. The FRC should regularly reevaluate these portfolio restrictions to align them with evolving market conditions.

Retail investor base. The establishment of the OTC market has effectively broadened market participation among professional investors, including high-net-worth individuals. However, to expand participation to retail investors, existing tax incentives for investment funds could be better promoted and financial literacy programs could be enhanced to educate retail investors about fixed-income products. Additionally, developing mechanisms that would allow retail investors to access the OTC bond market should be considered, either directly under appropriate investor protection frameworks or indirectly through collective investment vehicles.

Foreign investor base. Cumbersome paperwork creates a barrier for foreign investors seeking to open brokerage accounts. To encourage greater foreign participation in Mongolia's capital market, collaboration with relevant authorities including the MCSD is crucial. Streamlining the account opening process for foreign investors would significantly reduce this barrier and unlock their potential contribution to market development. To attract foreign investors to an LCBM, certain conditions must be met, including the creditworthiness of issuers, profitability, convenience, and effective risk management of investments. The creditworthiness of issuers and the profitability of local currency bonds are structural issues that are largely dependent on macroeconomic developments. Therefore, in the short term, the Mongolian capital market should focus on improving the convenience of foreign investment.

In this regard, global custodians should be established in Mongolia, using their own local branches or other local custodian banks ("sub-custodian" or "agent banks") with which they contract to be in their "global network" in each market to hold accounts for their respective clients. Global custodians offer foreign investors a comprehensive range of services, including custody, safekeeping, settlement, and administration of securities, as well as fund administration and compliance with local market regulations. Introducing omnibus accounts can provide foreign investors with easier access to the Mongolian securities markets. This would also eliminate the need for foreign investors to directly open a local brokerage account. To this end, the MCSD should be connected to international central securities depositories such as Clearstream and Euroclear to support cross-border transactions. However, it should be carefully designed with measures to address regulatory concerns arising from the anonymity of investors. Regarding risk management, an active secondary market with sufficient liquidity helps foreign investors cash out their investments.

Investor protection. While Mongolia's Civil Code and Bankruptcy Law provide clear definitions for defaulting payment obligations, there could be benefits to further enhancing investor protection in the specific context of bond markets. For instance, regulatory updates could be considered to formally introduce and define the roles of bondholders' representatives or trustees, thereby ensuring alignment between the interests of the issuer and the bondholders. This would complement the existing legal framework by addressing the specific needs of bond market participants.

Table 4: Summary of Recommendations—Investor Base

Recommendation	Agency	Timing[a]
Promote investor protection and broaden the investor base.		
(i) Continue to leverage the amended Investment Fund Law and existing tax incentives to further develop diverse investor profiles, including various types of investment funds, asset management firms, and insurance companies to expand the investment base for corporate bonds. This should involve revising regulatory hurdles that limit insurance company investments and updating pension fund regulations to encourage their engagement in the market.	MOF, FRC	MT
(ii) Address the lack of professional investors and foreign investors by simplifying procedural obligations and facilitating the entry of global custodians, thereby making the market more accessible to international participants.	MOF, FRC	MT
(iii) Clarify the regulatory definitions of "listing" and "registration" to eliminate confusion and revise restrictions that prevent mutual funds from accessing the OTC bond market.	FRC	NT
(iv) Enhance financial literacy and retail investor education programs, focusing on raising awareness and understanding of fixed-income instruments.	FRC, MASD	MT
(v) Introduce a regulatory framework for bondholder representatives or trustees to strengthen investor protection in the bond market.	FRC	MT
(vi) Develop the legal, operational, and risk management framework needed to implement omnibus accounts and connect the MCSD to international central securities depositories such as Clearstream and Euroclear.	FRC, MCSD	MT

FRC = Financial Regulatory Commission, MASD = Mongolian Association of Securities Dealers, MCSD = Mongolian Central Securities Depository, MOF = Ministry of Finance, OTC = over-the-counter.

[a] NT = near term (within 1 year), MT = medium term (1–3 years).

Source: Authors.

Issuer Base

Potential Issuers

Following the IMF's EFF program (2016–2018), during which Mongolia halted its sovereign debt issuance to preserve fiscal health, the government successfully resumed domestic government bond issuance in April 2025. This resumption represents a significant milestone in developing the local bond market and establishing a government bond yield curve, which is crucial for the evolution of the broader bond market. The new unified issuance system, operating through the MSE's electronic platform, has eliminated previous inefficiencies and inconsistencies in the government bond market.

Prior to resumption, market participants relied heavily on commercial bank savings rates to price corporate bonds, granting commercial banks excessive influence over corporate financing costs and limiting most corporate bond maturities to under 2 years. The reestablishment of government bond issuance now provides a proper benchmark for pricing across the market, supporting longer-term financing options for corporate issuers.

The new government bond issuance framework addresses several previous systemic weaknesses. The unified electronic platform eliminates the previous dual-venue structure that resulted in the same government bonds receiving different International Securities Identification Numbers based on the issuing market. The biweekly auction schedule with standardized procedures provides transparency and reduces risks of investor collusion that previously threatened appropriate benchmark interest rate settings.

Central bank bond issuances, which are short-term and used primarily as monetary policy tools, continue to serve these objectives, while the parallel development of the government bond market now provides the foundation for a comprehensive risk-free bond market across different maturities.

The introduction of the OTC market in September 2021 has provided companies with an alternative avenue for raising capital through bond issuances. While the OTC market is currently limited to professional investors, the issuance process has been significantly streamlined, enabling companies to issue corporate bonds within 1 to 2 weeks, compared to the 2 to 4 months typically required for public corporate bond issuances on the MSE.

This increased efficiency and flexibility have fueled remarkable growth in corporate bond issuances on the OTC market since 2021. Notably, the OTC corporate bond trading volume has surpassed the total trading volume of all securities on the MSE, effectively becoming the largest securities trading venue in Mongolia.

Securitization

Securitization was introduced in Mongolia following the enactment of the Asset-Backed Securities Market Law in 2011. The FRC updated its Regulation on Issuing, Registering, and Licensing of Asset-Backed Securities in 2022 and streamlined the process, leading to recent increases in public issuances of asset-backed securities (ABS) on the MSE in recent years. ABS has become the third most traded type of security on the MSE, trailing only stocks and corporate bonds. It accounted for 10.4% of the exchange's total trading volume in 2024. However, almost all ABS issuances have been issued by nonbank financial institutions, highlighting the need for a more diverse issuer base.

Credit Assessment

The Securities Market Law encompasses credit rating agencies (CRAs) within its purview, with the FRC's Regulation on Granting Licenses and Registration of Credit Rating Agencies (2010) and Regulation on Credit Rating Activities (2013) providing specific guidance. The recent amendments to the Securities Market Law have further emphasized the importance of CRAs by giving issuers a choice between obtaining a guarantee or a credit rating for proposed corporate bond issuances. This regulatory enhancement aims to strengthen risk assessment in the market and provide investors with more transparent information about issuers' creditworthiness.

The first credit-agency-rated bond was publicly issued on the MSE in October 2023. As of December 2024, 11 credit-agency-rated bonds had been issued, both publicly and privately, in the Mongolian bond market.

Assessment and Recommendations: Issuer Base

Potential issuers. With the successful resumption of government bond issuance in April 2025, the focus has shifted from re-issuance planning to optimizing the ongoing issuance program and fostering broader market development. The new unified electronic platform and biweekly auction schedule provide a solid foundation for continued market growth. Key considerations for further development include:

(i) **Further develop the current system for issuing government bonds.** This could be done by instituting a primary dealer system, adjusting maturity periods to better meet market demands, and establishing secondary market development incentives including market-making commitments from primary dealers, liquidity provision requirements, and performance-based allocation benefits that reward active secondary market participation and price discovery contributions.

(ii) **Develop a benchmark issues across the yield curve.** This should be the focus as the government bond market matures, along with ensuring sufficient liquidity in secondary markets. The current biweekly schedule provides regular supply, but attention to building fungible benchmark issues will enhance the market's utility as a pricing reference for corporate bonds.

(iii) **Diversify the investor base.** Medium-term strategies should look beyond commercial banks to include entities with varying risk appetites, such as mutual funds, pension funds, and insurance companies. With securities companies already participating in the government bond market through the MSE platform, focus should shift to encouraging their active role in **developing repo markets** and fostering more active secondary trading. Unlike banks, securities firms have incentives to develop trading-oriented business models that enhance overall market liquidity.

(iv) **Promote regulatory certainty and continued support for OTC bond issuance.** This will help to sustain the market's growth trajectory and maintain its advantages for issuers. The OTC market's efficiency in enabling corporate bond issuance within 1 to 2 weeks has made it the largest securities trading venue in Mongolia by volume. Continued regulatory flexibility should be balanced with appropriate monitoring of issuance practices to ensure investor protection standards and market integrity are maintained while preserving the streamlined processes that have driven market growth.

Securitization. It is important to define the concepts of "true sale" and "bankruptcy remoteness" in the Securities Market Law in close relation to Mongolia's bankruptcy regime. If the transfer of underlying assets from an originator to a special-purpose vehicle is viewed by the bankruptcy court as a secured loan instead of a true sale, the assets will become part of the originator's bankruptcy estate, leading to legal instability and costly problems for investors.

CRAs. The introduction of CRAs and credit-agency-rated bonds marks a positive development in Mongolia's market. The recent amendments to the Securities Market Law, which emphasize the role of CRAs by allowing issuers of corporate bonds to choose between obtaining a guarantee or a credit rating, represent a significant step forward. This regulatory enhancement should help improve transparency and risk assessment in the market. However, given that only 11 bonds are currently credit-rated out of hundreds issued in the market, strengthening the capabilities and expanding the role of credit rating agencies is essential to stimulate market growth and provide investors with diversified risk assessments.

Table 5: Summary of Recommendations—Issuer Base

Recommendation	Agency	Timing[a]
Optimize government bond market development and enhance market participation.		
(i) Further develop the current system for issuing government bonds by instituting a primary dealer system, adjusting maturity periods to better meet market demands, and establishing secondary market development incentives including market-making commitments from primary dealers, liquidity provision requirements, and performance-based allocation benefits that reward active secondary market participation and price discovery contributions.	MOF	MT
(ii) Focus on developing benchmark issues across the yield curve as the government bond market matures, ensuring sufficient liquidity in secondary markets and building fungible benchmark issues to enhance the market's utility as a pricing reference for corporate bonds.	MOF	NT
(iii) Diversify the investor base for government bonds beyond commercial banks to include entities with varying risk appetites, such as mutual funds, pension funds, and insurance companies. Encourage securities companies to take an active role in developing repo markets and fostering more active secondary trading to enhance overall market liquidity.	MOF, FRC	MT
(iv) Promote regulatory certainty and continued support for over-the-counter bond issuance to sustain access for issuers and reduce the time to market, while maintaining investor protection standards.	FRC, MASD	MT
(v) Define "true sale" and "bankruptcy remoteness" under the Securities Market Law to provide a stable legal basis for securitization transactions in line with international practices.	FRC	MT
(vi) Support the development of credit rating agencies through capacity building, technical assistance, and implementation of rating quality standards to ensure meaningful and trusted credit assessments in the bond market.	FRC	MT

FRC = Financial Regulatory Commission, MASD = Mongolian Association of Securities Dealers, MOF = Ministry of Finance.

[a] NT = near term (within 1 year), MT = medium term (1–3 years).

Source: Authors.

Intermediation

Intermediaries: Brokers and Dealers

In Mongolia's capital market, securities companies act as intermediaries, with their operations and licensing overseen by the FRC Regulation on Conducting Regulated Activities in the Securities Market (updated in 2023).

Despite several positive market developments and new entrants into the Mongolian capital markets, the regulatory framework concerning brokerage firms and underwriters' qualifications has not been sufficiently updated. The current minimum capital requirement stands at MNT100 million for brokerage licenses and MNT1 billion for underwriting licenses. This has led to operationally suspended brokerage firms continuing to exist while hampering market development by failing to keep up with new infrastructure system updates. Out of 55 brokerage firms licensed by the FRC, less than half are actively operating, leaving a significant number registered but inactive. This inactivity hinders market infrastructure providers from implementing system upgrades and excludes many market participants from advancements. Feedback from market infrastructure providers highlights this as a key barrier to transitioning to fully digital operations, necessitating the continued use of paper forms in various MCSD operations.

Mongolia has not yet adopted a primary dealer system for the distribution and trading of government bonds.

Trading Platforms

The bond market in Mongolia is segmented into exchange and OTC markets. The exchange market primarily operates through the MSE, which utilizes the Millennium IT system, an electronic trading platform developed by a company from Sri Lanka. The OTC market is managed by the MASD, which uses the locally developed M-OTC trading system.

Each of these systems presents distinct advantages and challenges:

(i) **The MSE trading system:**

- The MSE trading system, currently used for issuing and trading government bonds, is now outdated and cannot be updated further. This is because the developer no longer exists and the MSE does not have the source code.
- As a government-owned entity, the MSE must carefully consider various factors when selecting a system developer, with a strong emphasis on maintaining fairness and transparency in its procedures. The selection process must strike a balance between technical capabilities, cost-effectiveness, alignment with national interests, and the system's potential for future upgrades and enhancements.
- The government favors using the MSE for issuing government bonds as it would be a good revenue driver for the state-owned exchange. However, the outdated system remains a significant hurdle.

(ii) **The MASD trading system:**

- The M-OTC trading system offers significant advantages over the MSE. It provides a fully digitalized and online environment for the entire life cycle of securities, encompassing registration, trading, and settlement. It also boasts faster settlement times, offering either T+0 or T+1, compared to the standard T+2 settlement time frame on the MSE.
- Being locally developed, the system's main advantage is its high degree of customizability and rapid adaptability to local market needs. Unlike foreign-developed systems that often require additional development for local customization, this system can be quickly modified to meet the specific requirements of the Mongolian market. The speed of development and potential cost savings in ongoing customization are additional beneficial factors.
- However, as an OTC trading system, it is accessible only to professional investors rather than retail participants, and currently facilitates trading of corporate bonds, with government bonds not yet traded on this platform.
- The system is operated by the MASD, which is independent of the government, potentially reducing government incentives to choose it as the venue for government bond trading.

These combined factors have propelled the M-OTC platform to become the leading venue for corporate bond trading in Mongolia's capital market.

Transparency of Trading and Pricing

Trades on both the MSE and the OTC platforms are disclosed on their respective websites. However, the information available to the public on the OTC platform website is considerably less comprehensive than the information provided by the public exchange. This is because the OTC market is restricted to professional investors, who have access to more extensive and privileged information that is not shared on the platform's public website. There is no separate platform dedicated to post-trade transparency.

Assessment and Recommendations: Intermediation

Intermediaries. The corporate bond market, despite having over 50 brokerage firms, is hindered by outdated, paper-based processes and a lack of confidence from settlement banks in local brokers, stalling market progress. Only 15 firms are active in the OTC bond market, with just a few capable of investing in system improvements and adapting to market changes. This challenge is exacerbated by the requirement for pre-funding bond transactions.

To address the issue of inactive brokerage firms, the FRC should implement a multifaceted approach that combines regulatory incentives, technological support, and market-based solutions. A "tier-based" licensing system could be introduced, where brokerage firms are categorized based on their operational capabilities, capital adequacy, and technological readiness. This would create clear pathways for inactive firms to resume operations at an appropriate level while ensuring market integrity.

For firms unable to meet the updated requirements, a time-bound restructuring or consolidation framework should be developed to encourage mergers or acquisitions among brokerage firms, thereby creating stronger entities that can meet modern market demands.

A primary dealer system aligned with local market conditions should be introduced, and a specialized secondary market for government bonds established. In the government bond sector, the absence of a primary dealer system results in a limited active secondary market for government bonds. With the successful resumption of government bond issuance, implementing a primary dealer framework would enhance market-making capabilities, improve liquidity provision, and strengthen the overall functioning of the government bond market.

Mechanisms to safely broaden retail investor access to OTC bond markets should be evaluated to enhance retail bond market development and increase market competition. Currently, retail investors are excluded from the OTC market, which limits retail participation in the largest bond trading venue by volume and restricts their access to the streamlined corporate bond issuance process that has driven market growth.

Trading platforms. A disconnect in long-term strategy and coordination among financial market infrastructures (FMIs) has led to staggered system upgrades and barriers to development, particularly for the MSE, which relies on systems developed by an international IT firm. Establishing early-stage coordination among all market stakeholders (including the BOM, the MCSD, the MSCC, and the MSE) is crucial for harmonious system design and implementation.

Transparency of trading and pricing. Enhancing transparency is pivotal for attracting foreign investment to Mongolia's capital market. To increase the transparency of trading in the bond market, an organization that provides reliable bond price information should be established. The reliability of bond prices is an important factor in the development of the bond market. However, since not all bonds are traded daily, there are limitations to increasing stakeholder confidence in bond prices. In addition, Mongolia's investment firms are small and have limited dealing capabilities, making it difficult to provide reliable price information. Therefore, it is necessary to consider the introduction of an organization that aggregates bond trading information and calculates fair market prices based on theoretical pricing. A bond fair market value calculation organization is an organization that collects all types of price information and calculates and publishes prices by type based on this information. The introduction of such an organization and the obligation for financial institutions to utilize such information when calculating the repurchase price of investment instruments will introduce reasonable market prices and enhance price transparency in the bond market.

Table 6: Summary of Recommendations—Intermediation

Recommendation	Agency	Timing[a]
Consider introducing a primary dealer system for government bonds and raise qualifications requirements for securities companies.		
(i) Introduce a primary dealer system aligned with local market conditions and establish a secondary market for government bonds to improve the efficiency of issuance and trading in the Mongolian government bond market.	MOF, FRC	MT
(ii) Enhance intermediary credibility by introducing regulations that permit only investment banks with strong creditworthiness and technological capabilities to underwrite and broker corporate bonds. Reevaluate minimum capital requirements and accelerate the transition from paper-based processes through synchronized system enhancements across market participants.	FRC, MCSD	NT
(iii) Implement a tier-based licensing system for brokerage firms based on operational capabilities, capital adequacy, and technological readiness. Establish technical assistance programs for inactive firms and develop consolidation frameworks for firms unable to meet updated requirements.	FRC, MASD	NT
(iv) Explore options to broaden safe retail investor access to over-the-counter bond instruments, potentially through mutual funds, investment platforms, or fintech channels.	FRC, MASD	MT
(v) Establish a framework for reliable bond pricing using independent pricing services or credit rating agencies to strengthen transparency and investor confidence.	FRC, MASD, local credit rating agency	MT

FRC = Financial Regulatory Commission, MASD = Mongolian Association of Securities Dealers, MCSD = Mongolian Central Securities Depository, MOF = Ministry of Finance.

[a] NT = near term (within 1 year), MT = medium term (1–3 years).

Source: Authors.

ASSESSMENT SUMMARY AND ROAD MAP

3

Summary of Assessment and Recommendations

The country assessment conducted a gap analysis against the desired situation for bond market development in Mongolia. Mongolia has gaps in each of the dimensions considered, with investor base having the largest gap and financial market infrastructure having the smallest. These gaps should not be seen as limitations that prevent the realization of the preferred scenario, but rather as areas where further improvements are suggested for the development of Mongolia's bond market.

Figure 2: Results of the Assessment of the Mongolian Bond Market

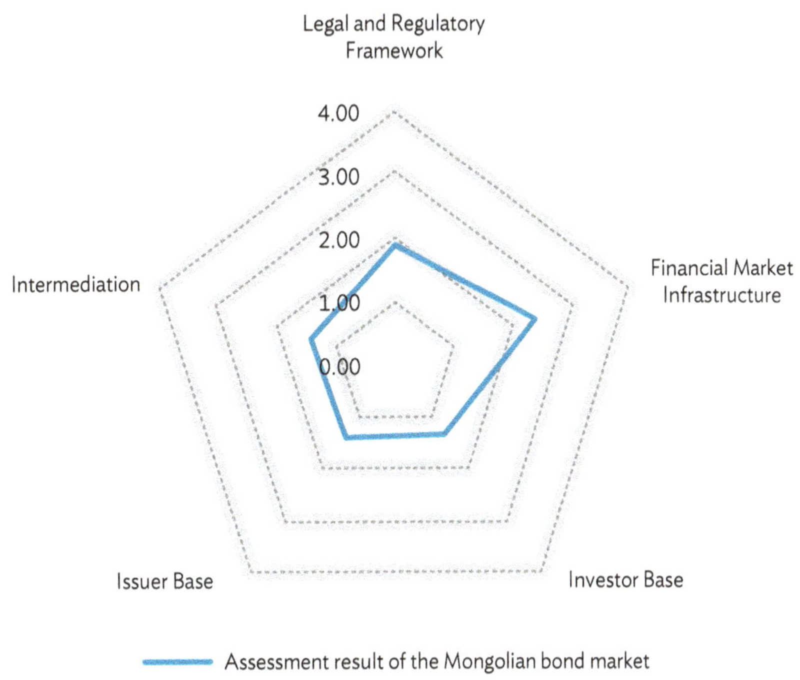

Source: ADB consultant.

Based on the assessment in this report, the ADB technical assistance team has prioritized recommendations for each subdimension to ensure efficient implementation. These priorities were set based on the team's experience studying the development processes of local currency bond markets (LCBMs) in major countries.

Table 7: Priorities of Recommendations

Dimension (5)	Subdimension (18)	Recommendation	Priority (Executive Summary)
1. Legal and regulatory framework	1.1. Long-term development plan for capital markets	☐ **Develop a comprehensive bond custodian regime** aligned with the amended Securities Market Law that establishes clear custody arrangements facilitating cross-border investment flows.	R1(iv)
		☐ **Support the creation of a government bond yield curve** and enable the development of a secondary market and instruments such as securities lending and repo.	R1(iv)
	1.2. Overall bond market	☐ Building on the amended Securities Market Law, develop FRC regulations to provide more detailed provisions addressing **bond defaults and cross-default situations**, drawing on international examples from civil law jurisdictions such as France, Germany, and the Republic of Korea.	R1(i)
		☐ Implement a regulatory framework to oversee the appointment and functioning of **bondholders' representatives or trustees**, ensuring alignment with bondholders' interests.	R1(ii)
		☐ Clarify and strengthen the **governance and oversight framework for self-regulatory organizations** to ensure consistency in delegated regulatory functions and accountability aligned with international best practices.	R1(vi)
		☐ Harmonize terminology in relevant laws and regulations to **standardize the use of "bond"** across legal documents and align with international market conventions and investor expectations.	R1(vii)
	1.3. Primary bond market	☐ **Continue refining the operational frameworks** of financial market infrastructures to fully implement the provisions of the amended Securities Market Law, particularly those related to **clearing, settlement, and custody services.**	R1(iii)
	1.4. Secondary bond market	☐ **Update key regulations and systems of the financial market infrastructures** to reflect recent changes in bond market registration regulations and increased market demand.	
	1.5. Green, social, and sustainability bonds	☐ **Review the regulatory framework for green, social, and sustainability bonds** once sufficient market data is available to assess its effectiveness.	R1(v)

continued on next page

Table 7 *continued*

Dimension (5)	Subdimension (18)	Recommendation	Priority (Executive Summary)
2. Financial market infrastructures	2.1. Authorities for financial market infrastructures	☐ To enhance the efficiency of post-trade operations in the Mongolian securities market, establish and operate a committee tentatively named the **"Capital Market Efficiency Committee."**	R2(i)
		☐ Strengthen the coordination function of the **Financial Market Stability Council** to align national financial market infrastructures' modernization efforts and ensure regulatory coherence across financial market infrastructures and supervisory bodies.	R2(ii)
	2.2. Central securities depository/ Securities settlement system	☐ Bolster capital market infrastructure by supporting the Mongolian Central Securities Depository to either migrate to the Bank of Mongolia's **DEPO/X system or develop/procure its own IT system** to replace the outdated IT infrastructure, prioritizing the option that best serves long-term operational efficiency and customization needs.	R2(iii)
		☐ Validate the **effectiveness of the current delivery versus payment model** and implement a delivery versus payment framework aligned with the Principles for Financial Market Infrastructures to efficiently manage principal risk in the capital market.	R2(v)
		☐ Foster qualitative growth in Mongolia's capital markets by reviewing the **introduction of liquidity provision mechanisms** such as securities lending and borrowing and tri-party repo, ensuring efficient implementation in conjunction with new IT system adoption.	R2(vi)
	2.3. Central counterparty	☐ Review the introduction of a **central counterparty system** to efficiently manage credit risk in the capital market, including the adoption of legal frameworks and risk management systems aligned with the Principles for Financial Market Infrastructures.	R2(iv)
3. Investor base	3.1. Institutional investor base	☐ Continue to leverage the amended Investment Fund Law and existing tax incentives to **further develop diverse investor profiles**, including various types of investment funds, asset management firms, and insurance companies to expand the investment base for corporate bonds. This should involve **revising regulatory hurdles** that limit the range of instruments available for insurance company investments and updating pension fund regulations to allow pension funds to purchase corporate bonds and actively participate in the market.	R3(i)

continued on next page

Table 7 *continued*

Dimension (5)	Subdimension (18)	Recommendation	Priority (Executive Summary)
		☐ Clarify the **regulatory definitions of "listing" and "registration"** to eliminate confusion and revise restrictions that prevent mutual funds from accessing the over-the-counter bond market.	R3(iii)
	3.2. Retail investor base	☐ Enhance **financial literacy and retail investor education** programs, with a focus on raising awareness and understanding of fixed-income instruments.	R3(iv)
	3.3. Foreign investor base	☐ Address the lack of professional investors and foreign investors by **simplifying procedural obligations and facilitating the entry of global custodians**, thereby making the market more accessible to international participants.	R3(ii)
		☐ Develop the legal, operational, and risk management framework needed to implement omnibus accounts and **connect the Mongolian Central Securities Depository to international central securities depositories such as Clearstream and Euroclear**.	R3(vi)
	3.4. Investor protection	☐ **Introduce a regulatory framework for bondholder representatives or trustees** to strengthen investor protection in the bond market.	R3(v)
4. Issuer base	4.1. Potential Issuers	☐ Further develop the current system for issuing government bonds by instituting a **primary dealer system** that is adaptable to market conditions, adjusting maturity periods to better meet market demands, and establishing secondary market development incentives including market-making commitments from primary dealers, liquidity provision requirements, and performance-based allocation benefits that reward active secondary market participation and price discovery contributions.	R4(i)
		☐ Focus on developing **benchmark issues across the yield curve** as the government bond market matures, ensuring sufficient liquidity in secondary markets and building fungible benchmark issues to enhance the market's utility as a pricing reference for corporate bonds.	R4(ii)

continued on next page

Table 7 *continued*

Dimension (5)	Subdimension (18)	Recommendation	Priority (Executive Summary)
		☐ **Diversify the investor base for government bonds** beyond commercial banks to include entities with varying risk appetites, such as mutual funds, pension funds, and insurance companies. Encourage securities companies to take an active role in developing **repo markets** and fostering more active secondary trading to enhance overall market liquidity.	R4(iii)
		☐ Promote regulatory certainty and continued **support for over-the-counter bond issuance** to sustain access for issuers and reduce the time to market, while maintaining investor protection standards.	R4(iv)
	4.2. Securitization	☐ Define **"true sale" and "bankruptcy remoteness"** under the Securities Market Law to provide a stable legal basis for securitization transactions in line with international practices.	R4(v)
	4.3. Credit rating agencies	☐ Support **the development of credit rating agencies** through capacity building, technical assistance, and implementation of rating quality standards to ensure meaningful and trusted credit assessments in the bond market.	R4(vi)
5. Intermediation	5.1. Intermediaries: Brokers and dealers	☐ Introduce a **primary dealer system** aligned with local market conditions and establish a specialized secondary market for government bonds to improve the efficiency of issuance and trading in the Mongolian government bond market.	R5(i)
		☐ Enhance the credibility of intermediaries by introducing regulations that permit only investment banks with strong creditworthiness and technological capabilities to underwrite and broker corporate bonds. **Reevaluate minimum capital requirements** and accelerate the **transition from paper-based processes** through synchronized system enhancements across market participants.	R5(ii)
		☐ **Implement a tier-based licensing system for brokerage firms** based on their operational capabilities, capital adequacy, and technological readiness, along with a technical assistance program to help inactive firms upgrade their systems and develop consolidation frameworks for firms unable to meet updated requirements.	R5(iii)

continued on next page

Table 7 *continued*

Dimension (5)	Subdimension (18)	Recommendation	Priority (Executive Summary)
	5.2. Trading platforms	☐ Explore options to broaden safe **retail investor access to over-the-counter bond** instruments, through mutual funds, investment platforms, or fintech channels.	R5(iv)
	5.3. Transparency of trading and pricing	☐ Establish a framework for reliable bond pricing using **independent pricing services** or **credit rating agencies** to strengthen transparency and investor confidence.	R5(v)

FRC = Financial Regulatory Commission, IT = information technology.

Source: ADB consultant.

Road Map for Local Currency Bond Market Development in Mongolia

The recommendations above are anticipated to contribute to the development of the LCBM in Mongolia. The expected effects concerning the dimensions of bond market development include an overall enhancement in the bond market institutional framework through improvements in the legal and regulatory aspects. Additionally, improvements in the reliability and efficiency of bond trading are expected through enhancements in financial market infrastructures (FMIs). Building upon these institutional improvements, both the primary and secondary markets are likely to grow. Ultimately, as investors' confidence in the bond market increases, the investor base is expected to broaden. If concerted efforts are made to implement these recommendations, the Mongolian bond market is anticipated to improve as illustrated in Figure 3.

Figure 3: Status and Road Map

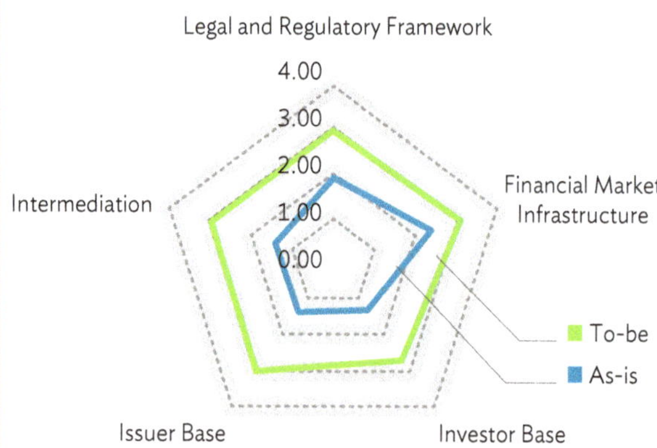

Source: ADB consultant.

APPENDIX 1

FINANCE SECTOR ASSESSMENT

Macro Financial Developments

Mongolia's economic landscape has undergone a transformative shift with the advent of foreign direct investment in its abundant mineral resources, such as copper, gold, and coal. This shift has moved the economy away from its traditional reliance on herding and agriculture, with exports now constituting a significant portion of gross domestic product (GDP). The country's trade is deeply interwoven with that of its neighbors, especially the People's Republic of China (PRC), which is the primary destination for the majority of Mongolian exports, and the Russian Federation, a crucial energy supplier. Such dependencies, however, expose Mongolia to external price shocks.

The withdrawal of Soviet support in the early 1990s led to a steep economic downturn, which was countered in the following years by substantial market reforms and privatization. Joining the World Trade Organization in 1997, Mongolia has since striven to integrate more deeply into regional and global economic networks. The establishment of a stock exchange and amendments to mining and investment laws have been steps toward stabilizing the investment climate and reviving economic growth.

From 2004 to 2008, Mongolia's economy expanded at an average annual rate of nearly 9%, driven by soaring global copper prices and increasing gold production. However, the 2008 global financial crisis impacted Mongolia, leading to a 1.3% shrinkage in its real economy in 2009. The $236 million Stand-by Arrangement provided early in 2009 by the International Monetary Fund (IMF) helped Mongolia emerge from the crisis with a stronger banking sector and better fiscal management. In October 2009, Mongolia passed long-awaited legislation on an investment agreement to develop the Oyu Tolgoi mine, one of the world's largest copper and gold deposits.

Nonetheless, investor disputes over the development of Oyu Tolgoi raised concerns about Mongolia's appeal to foreign investors, resulting in a marked decline in foreign direct investment and economic deceleration. Growth in the economy, which had surged above 10% annually from 2011 to 2013 due to robust commodity exports and government expenditure, slowed to 7.8% in 2014 and dipped to 2% in 2015. A rebound occurred from a short-lived 1.6% contraction in Q3 2016 to 5.8% in the first three quarters of 2017, largely due to rising commodity prices.

The 2015 Rio Tinto agreement to reinitiate operations at the Oyu Tolgoi mine, along with the associated $4.4 billion financing deal in December 2015, aimed to reverse faltering investor confidence. Facing a sharp decline in foreign direct investment, rising external debt, and a significant budget deficit, Mongolia negotiated a $5.5 billion financial aid package from the IMF and other international lenders in May 2017. This package aimed at bolstering Mongolia's long-term fiscal and economic health, contingent upon executing challenging reforms, such as merging the government's off-balance sheet liabilities and revamping the banking sector.

In 2020, the economy came to a standstill due to the global pandemic, resulting in a 4.6% contraction in GDP. While GDP growth rebounded to 7.4% in 2023, the slowdown in the PRC's economy and a decline in its raw material imports is a headwind in the near term.

Figure A1.1: GDP (in constant 2015 $) and GDP Growth (2024)

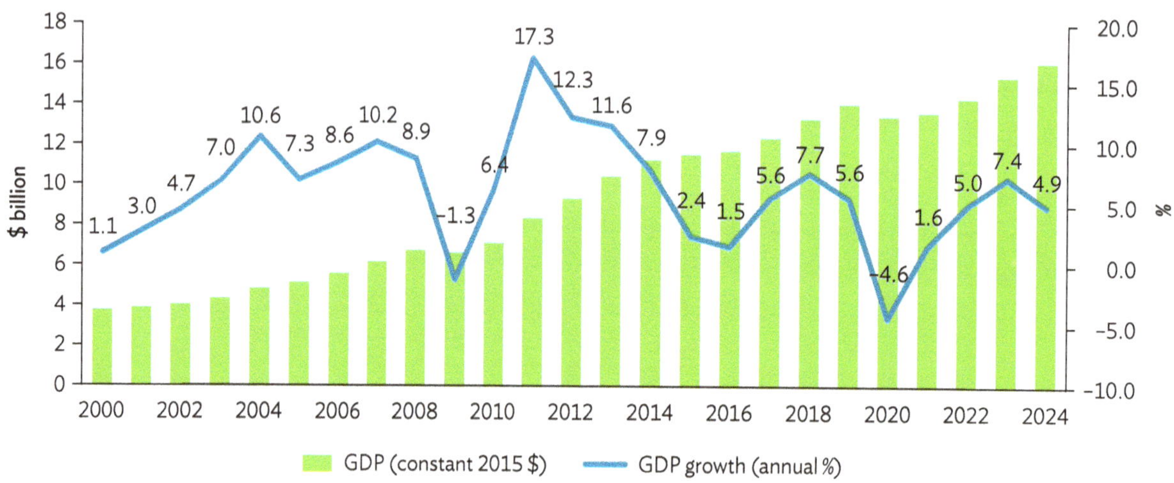

GDP = gross domestic product.
Sources: World Bank; National Statistics Office of Mongolia.

In recent years, Mongolia's economic landscape has become more dynamic, with the mining, agriculture, and service sectors substantially contributing to the country's GDP. The mining sector comprised 27% of GDP in 2024, and its influence on Mongolia's economic fluctuations is magnified by commodity cycles and the country's heavy reliance on the PRC as the primary market for its commodity exports.

Figure A1.2: GDP by Sector (2024)

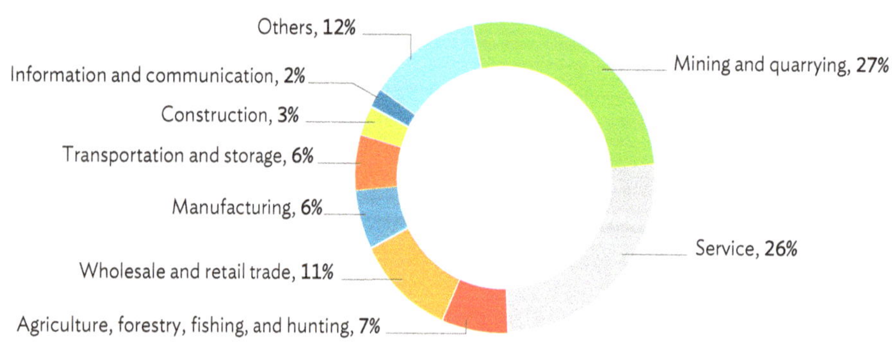

GDP = gross domestic product.
Source: National Statistics Office of Mongolia.

In 2024, Mongolia exported a total of $15.0 billion, representing a significant increase from previous years. The country saw its exports more than double in 5 years, increasing by $7.8 billion from $7.2 billion in 2020 to $15.0 billion in 2024. This significant expansion, predominantly driven by mineral exports, underscores Mongolia's strategic effort to attract foreign investment and capitalize on its abundant natural resources.

Coal constituted over half of these exports, valued at $8.7 billion or 58%, with copper concentrate at $3.3 billion or 22%, and gold at $0.9 billion or 6%. Additionally, iron ore contributed $598 million (4.0%), and crude oil accounted for $322 million (2.1%) of exports. A staggering 95% of Mongolia's total exports in 2024 were from the mining and precious metals sector, while textiles comprised a mere 2.4%.

Figure A1.3: Exports by Commodity (2024)

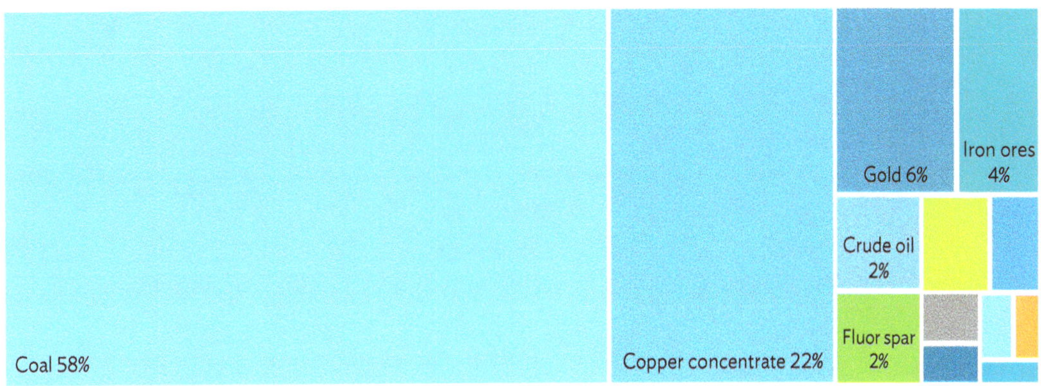

Source: National Statistics Office of Mongolia.

The PRC remains Mongolia's dominant export market, importing $14.4 billion worth of goods in 2024, accounting for an overwhelming 91% of Mongolia's total exports. While Mongolia has established trade relationships with other markets including Switzerland, the United States, Russia, and Iran, the country's export profile concentrates heavily on the Chinese market rather than diversifying, highlighting Mongolia's continued economic dependence on the PRC.

Figure A1.4: Exports by Destination (2024)

Source: National Statistics Office of Mongolia.

Driven by a surge in mineral exports, particularly coal, copper, and gold, Mongolia's trade balance has experienced a remarkable turnaround. After years of running trade deficits, the country's trade balance turned positive in 2014, and this positive trend has continued to gain momentum. In 2023, Mongolia's trade surplus reached an unprecedented level of $5.9 billion, marking a historical high.

This export-led growth has been accompanied by a substantial increase in the country's overall trade turnover. Over the past 5 years, Mongolia's total trade turnover has more than doubled, growing from $12.9 billion in 2020 to $27.4 billion in 2024. This surge in trade activity has been fueled by strong global demand for Mongolia's mineral resources, as well as the country's efforts to resolve its logistical issues in delivering the minerals to the PRC, its main export destination.

The robust trade performance has had a significant impact on Mongolia's foreign exchange reserves. As a result of the consistent trade surpluses and capital inflows, the country's foreign exchange reserves have reached historic highs. As of December 2024, Mongolia's foreign exchange reserves stood at $5.5 billion, providing a crucial buffer against external shocks and helping to ease pressures on the Mongolian togrog (MNT) exchange rate against major currencies, particularly the US dollar.

This sustained growth in trade and foreign exchange reserves has bolstered Mongolia's external position, enhancing its ability to service its external debt obligations and mitigating risks associated with currency volatility. However, the country's heavy reliance on mineral exports also underscores the need for economic diversification and continued efforts to foster a more resilient and sustainable growth model.

Despite recent improvements in trade performance and foreign reserves, in 2024 the International Monetary Fund (IMF) cautioned that procyclical fiscal expansion could jeopardize macroeconomic stability. Mongolia must pursue fiscal consolidation to rebuild sovereign buffers through improved tax administration, re-prioritized capital spending, and curbed wage-related expenditures. These reforms are essential to preserve debt sustainability and ensure resilience against external shocks.

Figure A1.5: Foreign Trade Turnover (2024)
($ million)

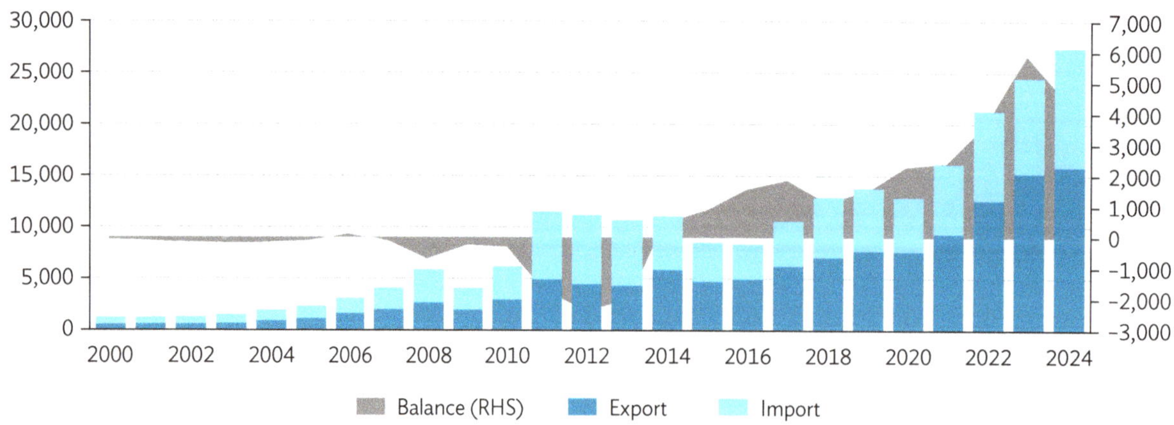

RHS = right-hand side.

Sources: National Statistics Office of Mongolia; Bank of Mongolia.

Figure A1.6: International Reserves and Exchange Rate (2024)

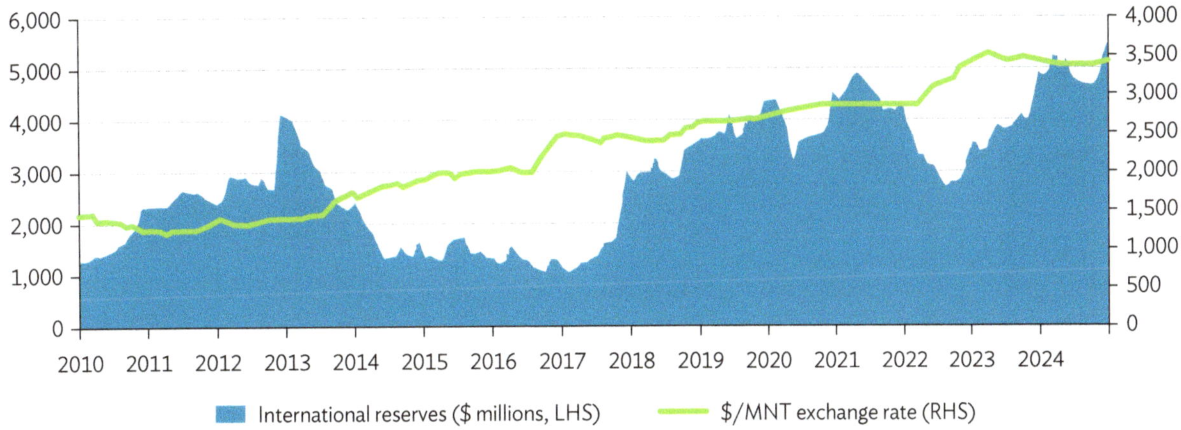

LHS = left-hand side, RHS = right-hand side.

Sources: National Statistics Office of Mongolia; Bank of Mongolia.

Although Mongolia operates under a floating foreign currency exchange rate regime, the central bank, the Bank of Mongolia (BOM), periodically intervenes in the foreign exchange market during periods of instability or market disruptions. Through transactions with local banks, the BOM aims to maintain a steady exchange rate for the Mongolian togrog, while still adhering to its primary objective of price stability. Despite these intermittent interventions, Mongolia's foreign exchange market remains largely open, with no capital controls or restrictions on foreign investment and trade flows.

However, the Government of Mongolia has implemented certain regulations concerning the use of foreign currencies within the country's borders. According to Article 4 of the Law on Conducting Settlements in National Currency (2009), the pricing of goods, works, and services must be denominated in Mongolian togrog, and all settlements within the territory of Mongolia must be conducted in the national currency. This law prohibits the setting of prices, conducting settlements, and advertising in foreign currencies or other settlement units without official approval from the BOM. Exceptions to this rule are granted for bank and nonbank financial institution loans, deposits, and related services.

In response to the economic challenges posed by the global coronavirus disease (COVID-19) pandemic, including rising inflation, declining international reserves, and currency exchange rate volatility, the government introduced temporary currency restrictions. The Law on Preventing, Fighting and Reducing the Negative Effects of the Coronavirus Infection (COVID-19) on the Society and Economy (2020) mandated that all bank transfers within the country be conducted exclusively in Mongolian togrog. This measure aimed to support the national currency and maintain financial stability during the crisis period. Notably, this currency restriction remains in force even today, despite the fact that foreign reserves have soared to unprecedented levels, rendering such restrictions unnecessary.

Mongolia has experienced mixed trends in inflation rates in recent years. According to the BOM, the December 2024 inflation rate was 8.4%, up from a low of 4.6% six months prior. This uptick follows a period of significant inflationary volatility, with rates reaching a peak of 16.1% in June 2022 before declining substantially. The global pandemic and subsequent economic disruptions contributed to the earlier inflation surge. While inflation decreased significantly from its 2022 peak, the recent increase to 8.4% suggests that inflationary pressures remain a concern, indicating that Mongolia continues to face challenges in maintaining consistent price stability despite progress made since the 2022 highs.

Figure A1.7: Inflation in Mongolia (2024)
(percentage)

Source: Bank of Mongolia.

Financial System Structure and Policies

Finance Sector Policies

Mongolia's finance sector remains relatively underdeveloped, with the banking sector playing a dominant role. According to the BOM, the banking sector constitutes about 90% of the finance sector in 2024. Despite recent growth in capital markets, the overall finance sector remains underdeveloped compared to more mature economies, with capital markets particularly lagging. This state can be attributed to several factors, including (i) the country's transition from a centrally planned economy to a market-based system following its independence from the Soviet Union in 1990, and (ii) the challenges posed by the highly cyclical nature of its mineral-dependent economy.

The Mongolian financial system is heavily bank-centric, with the banking industry accounting for the vast majority of financial intermediation. As of 2024, there were 14 commercial banks operating in Mongolia, including one state-owned bank and several foreign-owned institutions. The primary focus of these banks remains traditional deposit-taking and lending activities, with limited involvement in capital market financing or investment banking operations.

The finance sector is tightly regulated by the BOM and banks operate within a relatively restrictive regulatory environment. Financial literacy among the general population is low, although adoption of digital banking solutions is relatively high. The banking sector has historically grappled with high levels of nonperforming loans, prompting the BOM to implement various measures to improve asset quality and strengthen risk management practices. To address these persistent challenges, the IMF recommends regular asset quality reviews and strengthened provisioning standards. Additionally, stress testing for commodity-related and external shocks should be institutionalized to prevent the re-accumulation of systemic risks and ensure continued financial stability.

However, while the BOM plays a central role in monetary and financial stability, safeguards risks remain elevated due to weaknesses in BOM autonomy, transparency, and governance. Strengthening internal audit systems, enhancing external oversight, and increasing disclosure around reserve management operations would reinforce the central bank's credibility and operational soundness.

During the COVID-19 pandemic, the BOM initially lowered its policy interest rate to 6.0% in November 2020 in an effort to support the economy and boost borrowing. However, this accommodative policy stance was countered by a rise in global inflation, further amplified by domestic supply chain disruptions stemming from import restrictions with the PRC. By June 2022, inflation had surged to 16.1%. Faced with this inflationary crisis, the BOM swiftly reversed course, aggressively hiking its policy rate to 13.0% by December 2022 in a bid to rein in rising prices.

The central bank's tightening measures, coupled with the gradual easing of global supply constraints, have since contributed to lower inflation. As a result, the BOM has begun cautiously adjusting its monetary policy stance, lowering its policy rate to 10.0% in September 2024. While further rate cuts are anticipated as the central bank aims to support economic recovery, the trajectory of future policy actions will be closely tied to evolving inflationary pressures and the currency exchange rates.

Despite the success of the BOM's monetary tightening in containing inflation, the IMF cautions against procyclical risks if monetary loosening proceeds too quickly. To mitigate these risks, enhancing forward guidance and adopting a more rules-based monetary framework would help manage market expectations and preserve policy credibility.

Figure A1.8: Policy Interest Rate (2024)

(percentage)

Source: Bank of Mongolia.

Capital Market

While the banking sector dominates Mongolia's financial landscape, other segments remain underdeveloped. The capital markets, including the Mongolian Stock Exchange (MSE), is small and illiquid, with a limited number of listed companies (174 as of 2024) and low trading volumes (turnover ratio of 2.5% in 2024, according to the Financial Regulatory Commission [FRC]). The insurance industry, while growing rapidly in recent years, has yet to accumulate significant assets and plays a minor role in the overall financial system.

While equity market capitalization has grown significantly, nearly quadrupling over the past 5 years to reach MNT13.0 trillion in 2024, this growth is largely driven by regulatory actions rather than organic market development. A significant catalyst for this recent growth was the government's mandatory listing requirement for the five largest commercial banks by June 2023. These five banks now account for nearly half (45%) of the total market capitalization on the MSE after being listed between 2022 and 2023.

The development of a robust capital market was previously impeded by the absence of an active local currency government bond market. Mongolia had suspended sovereign debt issuance during the IMF's Extended Fund Facility program in 2017, with local currency government bond transactions effectively ceasing and the last trade occurring in 2019 when the 3-year government bonds matured. However, this situation changed significantly with the successful resumption of government bond issuance in April 2025. The Ministry of Finance restarted domestic government securities trading through a new unified electronic platform operating via the MSE, conducting biweekly auctions offering bonds across short-term (up to 1 year), medium-term (1–5 years), and long-term (over 5 years) maturities. This resumption represents a crucial milestone in establishing a reliable government bond yield curve, which serves as an essential benchmark for pricing other instruments in the capital market and supports the broader development of Mongolia's debt capital markets.

Figure A1.9: Market Capitalization and Trading Volume (2024)

(MNT billion)

RHS = right-hand side.

Source: National Statistics Office of Mongolia.

Despite the recent surge in market capitalization driven by bank listings, Mongolia's capital markets remain relatively underdeveloped. The lack of government bond issuance and trading activity, coupled with low stock trading volumes, underscores the need for further efforts to deepen and diversify the country's capital markets. Fostering a more vibrant and liquid capital market is essential to support long-term economic growth and development in Mongolia.

Local Currency Bond Market

Mongolia's local bond market has experienced a significant boost in development over the last several years, primarily driven by various regulatory initiatives aimed at promoting corporate bond issuances. Notable among these measures are the Regulation on Debt Instrument Registration (2021) and the Regulation on Operation of the OTC Market (2020) issued by the FRC.

These new regulations targeted corporate bond issuances, effectively lowering the regulatory requirements and hurdles that issuers faced. As a result, public corporate bond issuances on the MSE have increased substantially since 2021, reflecting the positive impact of these regulatory reforms on market activity.

Furthermore, the introduction of the over-the-counter (OTC) market in September 2021 has provided companies with an alternative avenue for raising capital through bond issuances. While the OTC market is limited to professional investors, it has significantly streamlined the issuance process, enabling companies to issue corporate bonds within 1–2 weeks, compared to the 2–4 months typically required for public corporate bond issuances on the MSE.

Figure A1.10: Corporate Bond Volume (2024)
(MNT billion)

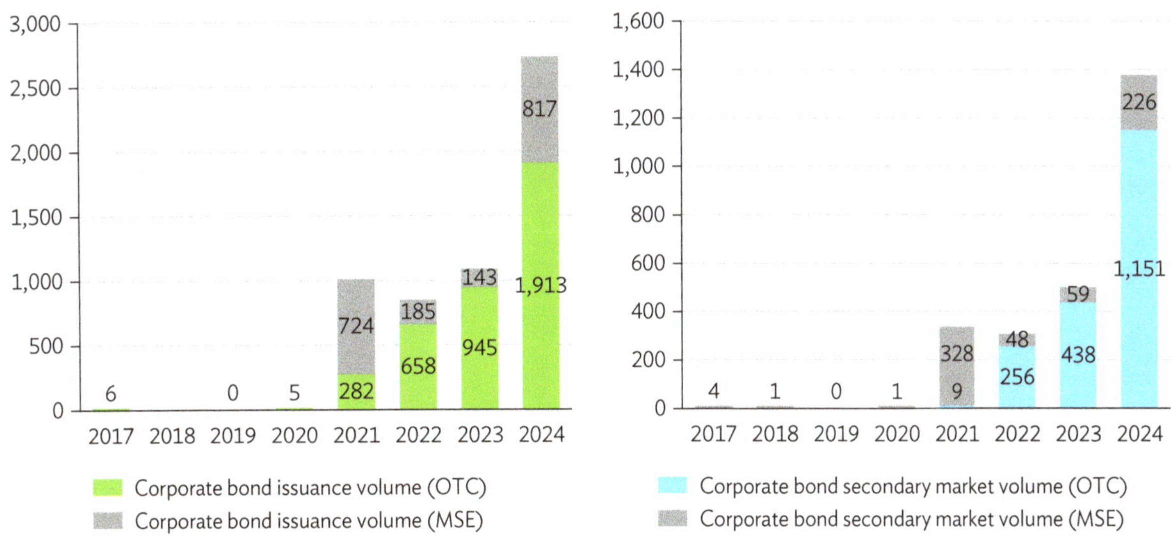

Sources: Mongolian Stock Exchange; Mongolian Association of Securities Dealers.

This increased efficiency and flexibility fueled remarkable growth in corporate bond issuances on the OTC market in 2022 and 2023. Notably, the OTC corporate bond trading volume has surpassed the total trading volume of all securities on the MSE, effectively becoming the largest securities trading venue in Mongolia. Since its inception, there have been more than 750 corporate bond issuances worth a staggering MNT3.8 trillion (approximately $1.1 billion) on the OTC market as of December 2024.

The surge in corporate bond issuances, facilitated by regulatory reforms and the introduction of the OTC market, has injected much-needed liquidity and depth into Mongolia's bond market. This influx of new corporate bond offerings has not only provided companies with alternative financing options but has also fostered increased trading activity in the secondary market.

Secondary market trading volume has picked up significantly, reaching as much as 38% of the total OTC bond market trading volume in 2024. This figure represents an increase from the 28% level observed throughout 2022, reflecting the growing vibrancy and liquidity of the OTC bond market.

In addition to the surge in trading activity, the OTC market has introduced several operational advantages that have contributed to its appeal among market participants. One notable benefit is the shorter settlement times offered on the OTC market, with the choice of T+0 (same-day settlement) and T+1 (next-day settlement), compared to the T+2 standard at the MSE. This improved settlement efficiency enables investors to manage their capital and deploy their cash resources in a timelier manner, enhancing their ability to capitalize on market opportunities more effectively.

Figure A1.11: OTC Corporate Bond Volume (2024)
(MNT billion)

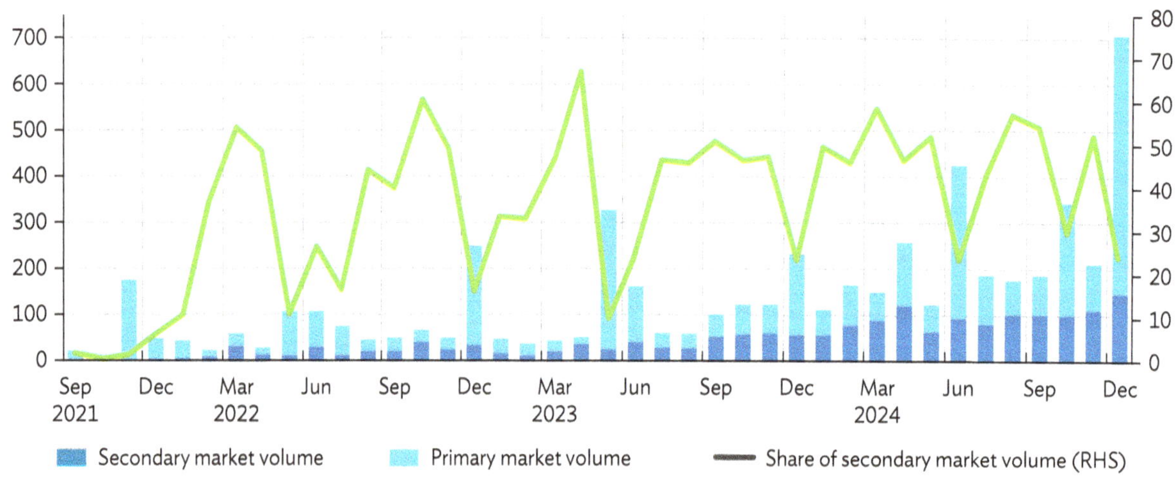

OTC = over-the-counter, RHS = right-hand side.

Source: Mongolian Association of Securities Dealers.

Another positive outcome of the robust trading activity on the OTC market has been the emergence of a yield curve for the Mongolian corporate bond market. Thanks to the ample volume and variety of different tenor bonds traded on the OTC platform, market participants now have access to a basic corporate bond yield curve. However, this yield curve primarily includes secured or credit-rated bonds, which may limit its effectiveness as a crucial benchmark for pricing all types of corporate bonds. The yield curve is preliminary, as it does not account for tenor differences within the same credit grade or spread differences between grades within the same tenor. Despite these limitations, the existence of this corporate bond yield curve is still significant.

Figure A1.12: OTC Corporate Bond Yield Curve (February 2024)

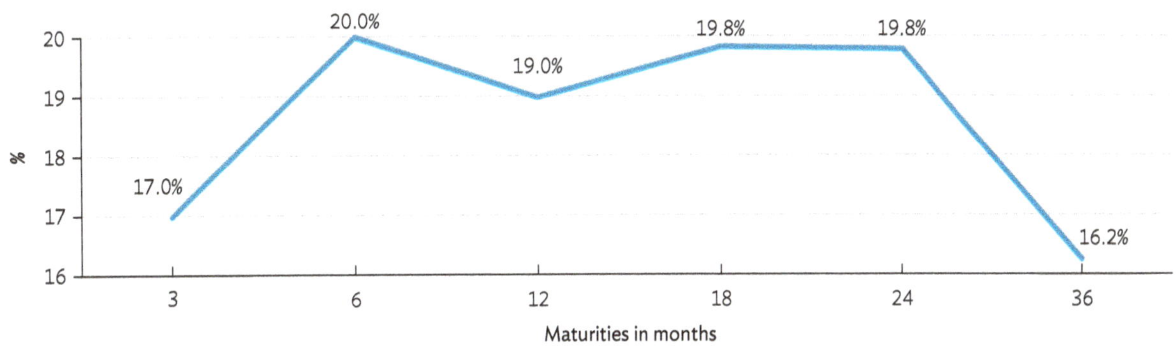

OTC = over-the-counter.
Source: Mongolian Association of Securities Dealers.

The emergence of the OTC market has not only facilitated corporate financing but has also fostered greater transparency, pricing efficiency, and liquidity in Mongolia's bond market.

Policy Initiatives for Capital Market Development

Since the publication of the Bond Market Guide for Mongolia in February 2021, the country's bond market has undergone significant regulatory changes aimed at improving efficiency, transparency, and accessibility. These reforms are part of a concerted effort by the authorities to foster a more conducive environment for issuers and investors, ultimately promoting the growth and development of Mongolia's debt capital markets.

FRC regulation on securities registration. One of the major changes was introduced through FRC Resolution No. 225 of 11 June 2021, which amended the Regulation on Securities Registration. Previously, this regulation mandated that publicly offered securities must have an asset valuation report prepared by a licensed valuation firm, a requirement that was considered unique and costly for the Mongolian bond market. However, the amended regulation has removed this mandatory requirement, allowing issuers to include an asset valuation report only if deemed desirable, thereby reducing the regulatory burden and associated costs.

FRC regulation on debt instrument registration. Another key development was the introduction of the Regulation on Debt Instrument Registration, as outlined in FRC Resolution No. 226 of 11 June 2021.

This regulation targets publicly offered debt instruments and provides less stringent requirements compared to initial public offerings. Prior to this regulation, the same strict requirements applied to both public companies and publicly offered debt instruments, creating unnecessary hurdles for bond issuances. Under the new regulation, publicly offered corporate debt instruments no longer require an independent valuation report or a legal opinion from a securities market-licensed valuation company or legal firm, streamlining the issuance process.

Securities Market Law revision. The Securities Market Law of Mongolia underwent much-anticipated revisions on 16 May 2024, updating the legislation to align with current market conditions and further enhancing the regulatory framework for the bond market and securities issuance process. These changes complement existing regulatory reforms and aim to create a more robust and flexible environment for debt capital markets. Key updates include:

(i) **Corporate bond issuance.** The revised law explicitly allows corporate bonds to be issued on both exchange and OTC markets, providing more flexibility for issuers and expanding potential market reach.

(ii) **Public offering requirements.** Publicly offered corporate bonds must now either be secured or guaranteed or have a credit rating from an authorized credit rating agency. This requirement enhances investor protection while maintaining flexibility for issuers.

(iii) **Streamlined bond programs.** Companies meeting certain criteria set by the FRC can now register their entire bond program at once, rather than registering each issue separately. This streamlined process reduces the administrative burden and allows for more efficient capital raising.

(iv) **Bank deposit certificates.** The revised law allows banks to issue deposit certificates for trading on the securities market, expanding the range of debt instruments available to investors.

(v) **Professional investor definition.** The definition of "professional investor" has been expanded to include investment banks, potentially broadening the institutional investor base for debt securities.

(vi) **Bondholder protection.** The revised law introduces a provision for enhanced bondholder protection. An authorized entity may now act on behalf of bondholders to safeguard their interests. This entity's powers include requesting pertinent information from the issuer, entering into collateral or guarantee agreements, and initiating legal proceedings to enforce bond obligations. This measure significantly strengthens the position of bondholders, particularly in cases of default or disputes, and aligns with international best practices in corporate governance and investor protection.

Faster approvals for high-quality issuers. The Regulation on Debt Instrument Registration also introduces a faster approval process for qualified issuers. Publicly offered corporate debt from high-quality issuers can now be approved within 10 business days, compared to the previous 20-day time frame. The criteria for a high-quality issuer include being listed on the main board of an exchange, ranking among the 100 largest business entities, or having a history of issuing public bonds (with at least two prior issuances). This expedited approval process incentivizes participation by established and reputable companies.

Bond issuance flexibility. The new regulation introduces the concept of bond issuance programs. Under this scheme, issuers can now spread out bond issuance across multiple tranches, requiring only a single registration approval from the FRC. This offers issuers greater flexibility in managing their financing needs.

A clear definition of "bond." The FRC Regulation on Debt Instrument Registration formally defines the term "bond" within the regulatory framework for the first time. Previously, the term "debt instrument" was used, leading to potential confusion and misuse by market manipulators. This clear definition promotes greater transparency and reduces the risk of market irregularities.

Green bond. The FRC has been working on expanding the scope of financial instruments available in the market by approving a regulation to foster the issuance and registration of green bonds. This initiative aligns with the international Green Bond Principles and aims to catalyze investments in environmentally sustainable projects, addressing the pressing need for a low-carbon, climate-resilient future in Mongolia.

Tax incentives. Complementing these regulatory reforms, the Government of Mongolia has introduced tax incentives to promote investments in publicly listed bonds. Specifically, the income tax on bond interest has been lowered from 10% to 5% for publicly listed bonds, making these investments more attractive to individual and institutional investors.

These comprehensive reforms, including the revision of the Securities Market Law, demonstrate Mongolia's commitment to developing a more sophisticated, efficient, and attractive bond market. By addressing key regulatory barriers, introducing new instruments, and aligning with international best practices, these initiatives are expected to stimulate both issuance and investment in Mongolia's debt capital markets.

While these capital market reforms represent significant progress, the broader economic context requires attention. Given the economy's continued dependence on mining exports, especially to the PRC, structural reforms to promote economic diversification remain essential. The IMF recommends advancing reforms to support small and medium-sized enterprise financing, value-added exports, and infrastructure development for non-mining sectors. These measures would reduce long-term economic fragility and create a more diversified foundation to support sustained capital market growth.

APPENDIX 2

DESIRABLE DISCIPLINES OF LOCAL CURRENCY BOND MARKETS

Capital Market

Capital market regulation can be categorized into economic regulation and prudential regulation.[1] Economic regulation refers to regulations that protect the domestic markets by restricting market entry or utilizing measures such as price controls to achieve macroeconomic objectives. While these regulations can be effective in achieving policy objectives or supporting domestic industries, they can also lead to inefficiencies and poor market practices. Prudential regulation is an approach to regulation that protects investors and reduces systemic risk by making financial markets fair, transparent, and efficient. Therefore, the direction of capital market-related regulatory improvements should focus on establishing an appropriate prudential regulatory framework that promotes market soundness with regulators integrating **technology-driven regulatory solutions (RegTech)**, **digital investor onboarding**, and the potential for **distributed ledger technology** in clearing and settlement as core components of capital market modernization to offer new tools for transparency, cost reduction, and oversight."

A key objective of capital market regulation is to establish efficient and transparent markets while promoting their sustainable development. To stimulate capital markets in developing countries, a regulatory system balancing enhanced transparency and market activity stimulation is essential. It is necessary to introduce a capital market system that considers market conditions while promoting policies to stimulate the market, alongside an appropriate regulatory framework for healthy capital market development. Effective capital market development requires a well-sequenced road map that considers the current level of financial development, institutional capacity, and economic structure. A strategy that phases reforms across foundational infrastructure, regulatory modernization, and investor and issuer capacity-building is critical to avoid premature liberalization or fragmented progress.

Regulation of capital markets is broader and more complex than that of banking and insurance. This is because banking and insurance regulation is focused on improving the asset quality of financial firms in the sector and protecting consumers, whereas securities market regulation involves intermediaries, stock exchanges, collective investment schemes, and issuers.

To introduce effective capital market regulation, it is necessary to define key terms, including securities, securities markets, market participants, and issuers, as appropriate to market conditions and to establish desirable norms for each of the market's key elements. It is also crucial to ensure that this institutional framework effectively operates in the market and serves as the basis for monitoring its performance.

---

1 B. Eschweiler. 2006. Bond Market Regulation and Supervision in Asia. *BIS Papers* No. 30.

For the healthy development of the capital market, an appropriate regulatory framework must be established to protect investors, ensure a fair and transparent market, and mitigate systemic risk. To this end, the concept and types of securities and derivatives should be defined, prudential regulation of market participants should be introduced, and a system for investor protection should be established. In addition, a system for introducing and regulating primary and secondary markets appropriate to the characteristics of each type of bond should be introduced, and a system for ensuring that market participants engage in fair and transparent trading should be established, as well as the requirements and operating systems for financial market infrastructures (FMIs).

Additionally, close coordination between financial regulators, central banks, and the finance ministry is vital for aligned capital market policies. Establishing formal interagency mechanisms can ensure consistent reform pacing, reduce regulatory overlap, and provide more coherent signaling to market participants.

Overall Bond Market

The development of a bond market requires the establishment of a legal and regulatory framework for securities, securities markets, and market participants that is appropriate to market conditions. Countries with developed bond markets are characterized by having in place comprehensive and flexible definitions of financial investment instruments, regulatory frameworks that align with the characteristics of the bonds, and bond market regulatory frameworks that enhance market transparency and fairness.

A crucial aspect of the legal and regulatory framework for bonds is that the country or regulator concerned must define bonds, regulate the issuance process, and establish a regulatory system to ensure a healthy market. Another element of the assessment is whether the legal and regulatory framework serves as a benchmark for the bond market and allows the market to operate properly. The definition of bonds should be broadly stated to include a range of instruments, including those with operational utility for money market and central bank policy objectives. A legal and regulatory framework should also serve as the basis for describing and regulating bond market activities and providing for supervision and enforcement. It is also essential to adopt a framework that is flexible enough to accommodate the addition of market functions, products, and processes as markets evolve. Most countries have adopted systems whereby the basic concepts and issuance procedures for bonds are outlined in civil, commercial, or capital markets legislation, while detailed standards for the markets and instruments are established in the individual laws governing the capital markets.[2]

The regulatory framework for bond markets should be designed to protect investors, ensure fairness and transparency for market participants, and minimize systemic risk for the national economy. A key element of the bond market regulatory framework is whether it is designed and operates to promote fairness and integrity. In this respect, the bond market regulatory framework is highly relevant to investor protection and requires high transparency for market participants.

2 The Securities Act of 1933 and Securities Exchange Act of 1934 in the United States, Markets in Financial Instruments Directive II (MiFiD II) and Markets in Financial Instruments Regulation (MiFIR) in the European Union, the Financial Instruments and Exchange Act in Japan, and the Financial Investment Services and Capital Markets Act in the Republic of Korea provide comprehensive regulatory frameworks for capital markets and financial investment products. For government bond issuance, the United States has the Treasury Bond Act, Japan has the Government Bond Act, and the Republic of Korea has the State Bond Act.

A clear regulatory framework regarding taxes is one of the most sensitive points for bond investors and is crucial for the development of capital markets. Tax incentives for bond investors (e.g., reduced withholding tax on interest income) and clear tax treatment for capital gains, coupons, and securitization vehicles can significantly boost participation, especially from institutional and foreign investors.

Primary Bond Market

Bond Issuance Process

Key concepts related to the primary market include the basis for issuance, registration, issuance procedures and regulations for public offerings and private placements, the issuance registration regimes for public offerings, including prospectuses, the underwriting functions of intermediaries, and the roles and functions of FMIs in the issuance process. Most countries have adopted strict regulatory frameworks for bond issuance. The regulation of issuance encompasses disclosure requirements for issuers and securities, issuance procedures, differentiated regulations for various types of offerings, including public offerings and private placements, as well as regulations governing the underwriting of securities.

The regulation of issuers and securities prescribes disclosure and reporting requirements for issuers in order to protect investors. It is essential that investors are informed of what they need to know to properly assess the risk associated with securities. The International Organization of Securities Commissioners' Objectives and Principles of Securities Regulation set out the principle that issuers should provide complete, accurate, and timely disclosure of financial results, risks, and other information that is material to investors' decision-making.

Regarding the issuance method, most countries have introduced differentiated regulations based on the method of placement (public offering or private placement). The criteria for distinguishing between public and private placements are generally based on the number of investors, the question of issuance to professional investors, capitalization, and trading volume. The method of solicitation results in differences in the issuance, distribution, and trading of securities offered to the public offerings. Most public offerings require a rigorous registration process with regulators. In some countries, the issuance and registration of bonds are conducted through stock exchanges rather than regulators, and a stock exchange may act as a self-regulatory organization.

In terms of issuance procedures, most countries have a registration process for public offerings, but the level of regulation of public offerings varies somewhat from country to country. For example, the United States (US) has very strict public offering procedures compared to Europe. In the US, as companies are reluctant to issue securities through the public offering process due to these strict public offering standards, the Rule 144A market has been introduced, which has a relatively relaxed disclosure process but limits the participating investors to professional investors only.

A desirable primary market regulatory framework is one in which detailed information about the issuer and its securities, including investment risks, is disclosed in a timely manner to protect investors, and the system must work well in practice. Additionally, transparent issuance procedures should enhance investor confidence, which is a crucial evaluation factor. In addition, it is also important to establish a system that suits the characteristics of the various securities and to differentiate subscription methods in accordance with the characteristics of investors. This differentiation should be based on these subscription methods, and various market structures should be introduced accordingly.

Government Bond Issuance System

The government bond market serves a variety of functions, including facilitating fiscal transfers, promoting financial market development, stabilizing economic fluctuations, financing economic development, and enhancing bond market development. In major countries, government bonds are mainly issued for fiscal transfers and to control economic fluctuations. In developing countries, however, the functions of financing economic development and promoting financial market development may be more important. In a bank-centered financial system, the ability of a country to raise funds for economic growth or fiscal conservation may be limited. Accordingly, countries are trying to develop government bond markets to facilitate long-term, large-scale financing for development and fiscal conservation.

Countries with large government bond markets are striving to build efficient primary and secondary markets in order to reduce financing costs and ensure timely funding. Major countries are introducing various policies to strengthen systematic government bond management in response to the increase in the size of government bond issuance and the diversification of government bond products and maturities.

Most countries operate a primary dealer system for the efficient issuance and distribution of government bonds. Primary dealers in each country are authorized to participate in government bond bidding, provided various benefits, and entrusted with market-making and information provision obligations. Primary dealers are also obliged to hold a certain level of government bonds for sale and to conduct a certain amount of trading, for example, in response to requests for trading in government bonds from general investors.

Secondary Bond Market

To vitalize the secondary bond market, it is essential to demonstrate the necessity and validity of introducing the secondary market, set standards for its operation, and implement a system to enhance transparency and efficiency in the market.

Secondary market regulation is introduced to create a market system that enables bonds to be traded smoothly and promotes price efficiency. In particular, the role of FMIs and transparent disclosure of trading information is important for a healthy secondary market.[3] Countries with active bond markets have institutional bases to enhance trading stability, systems of FMIs to ensure the proper operation of these markets, and proactive and reactive disclosure systems to enhance market efficiency and transparency.

To enhance liquidity in secondary markets, it may be necessary to introduce several proactive measures. For example, these could include implementing market-maker programs, enabling securities lending and borrowing, and establishing a government securities repo facility. These mechanisms help support price discovery and attract a more active investor base.

3 The pressing FMI function upgrade challenges facing the Mongolian securities market were proposed in the Working Paper for Mongolia, Project Number: 54122-001.

In terms of trading platforms, markets are organized in various ways. Most countries have introduced over-the-counter trading platforms,[4] while in some countries, stock exchanges provide trading platforms for certain bonds.[5] With different trading platform operators and management systems in different countries, the core of the regulations on trading platforms in major countries is aimed at enhancing pre- and post-trade transparency and improving the efficiency of the trading system to ensure smooth trading.

Green, Social, and Sustainability Bond Market

A green, social, and sustainability (GSS) bond is a bond issued to finance projects to improve various environmental and social conditions. Unlike ordinary bonds, GSS bonds are characterized by the fact that the funds raised through them can be used only for eligible projects aimed at improving specific environmental or social conditions.

For the issuance of GSS bonds, the International Capital Market Association sets out best practices in the **Green Bond Principles (GBP)**, which consist of **four core components** and **two key recommendations**.

Box A2.1: Green Bond Principles

Core components:

(i) **Use of proceeds:** The issuer shall adequately describe its plans for the use of the proceeds and the targeted environmental and social projects in all documents.

(ii) **Process for project evaluation and selection:** The environmental and social improvement objectives of the project, the procedure for determining whether the project is eligible, and the eligibility and selection criteria for the project shall be announced to investors.

(iii) **Management of proceeds:** The issuers should have procedures in place to manage proceeds, disclose the utilization of proceeds, and obtain an external audit of their internal methods of tracking proceeds and the allocation of proceeds.

(iv) **Reporting:** The issuer is obligated to provide investors, through an annual report, with up-to-date information on the use of the funds raised until the funds are fully utilized.

Key recommendations:

(i) **Use of frameworks:** Recommend the establishment and disclosure of a governing framework for bond issues.

(ii) **External reviews:** Encourage issuers to engage in ex ante reviews of their compliance with the Principles and ex post reviews of their management and use of the proceeds.

Source: International Capital Market Association.

GSS bonds have been growing strongly in volume every year since the first international organization issued a green bond in 2007. Major countries have announced carbon neutrality and inclusive growth strategies to combat climate change and have promoted the introduction of GSS bonds as a means of financing their implementation.

4 Bond trading is dominated by trades between professional investors, and most countries are thus characterized by trading platforms led by investment firms. However, in recent years, the share of trading on platforms led by information vendors such as Bloomberg has increased significantly.

5 The Republic of Korea government bonds are actively traded on the Republic of Korea Exchange's specialized government bond secondary market.

For green bonds to be introduced, a country must establish guidelines for their issuance that are in line with global standards. In addition, to determine the eligibility of a project for issuance of green bonds, a green taxonomy should be introduced that establishes economic activities appropriate to achieving environmental goals in consideration of the country's economy, industry, and social structure. Additionally, to facilitate the issuance of green bonds, a process for green bond certification and a follow-up monitoring system must be established.

In addition to use-of-proceeds instruments, **sustainability-linked bonds** are gaining traction globally. Sustainability-linked bonds allow greater issuer flexibility, linking bond terms (such as coupon step-ups) to the achievement of predefined environmental or social performance indicators. Introducing guidelines for these types of bonds can broaden the market and encourage issuer accountability.

Financial Market Infrastructures

Payment System

A payment system is a set of instruments, procedures, and rules for the transfer of funds between or among participants. The system includes the participants and the entity operating the arrangements.

The payment and settlement system can be classified into two categories: the large-value payment system, which handles interbank payments, and the retail payment system, which processes a large volume of low-value payments. The large-value payment system is called an interbank money transfer system because payments arising from funds, securities, or foreign exchange transactions are usually made between financial institutions. These payments involve large amounts per transaction, and given the time criticality of payment, the central bank operates the large-value payment system in most countries.

The stable functioning of an FMI for the clearing and settlement of securities requires stable operation of the funds transfer system. In particular, the central bank's large-value payment system is closely linked to other FMIs, as it carries out the final settlements of all transactions and may extend intraday liquidity to participating financial institutions.

A retail payment system handles low-value payments of companies or individuals and is characterized by a wide range of transaction users and a large number of payments. These retail payment services, in addition to mobile-based ones, used by the general public, are expected to be important channels for the direct execution of securities transactions.

Central Securities Depository and Securities Settlement Systems

A central securities depository provides securities accounts, central safekeeping services, and asset services, which may include the administration of corporate actions and redemptions and plays an important role in helping to ensure the integrity of securities issues.

The central securities depository is usually the operator of the securities settlement system and provides various settlement services by linking the securities settlement system and the payment system.
A securities settlement system enables securities to be transferred and settled by book entry in accordance with a set of predetermined rules. Securities settlement systems allow transfers of securities either free of payment or against payment. When a transfer is carried out against payment, many systems provide delivery versus payment services, where delivery of the securities occurs if and only if payment also occurs.

Central Counterparty

A central counterparty interposes itself between counterparties to contracts traded in one or more financial markets, acting as the buyer to every seller and the seller to every buyer, thereby ensuring the performance of open contracts. A central counterparty becomes the counterparty to trade with market participants through novation, through an open-offer system, or through an analogous legally binding arrangement. This makes central counterparties a vanguard in credit risk management, securing the stability and sustainable development of capital markets.

As capital markets mature, the introduction of derivatives such as interest rate swaps and foreign exchange forwards becomes increasingly important. These instruments allow investors and issuers to hedge interest rate and currency risks, thereby deepening market participation and enhancing pricing efficiency. Their development should be closely tied to FMI upgrades and regulatory oversight.

Investor Base

Institutional Investor Base

A stable investor base is important for the development of a bond market. The investor base is related to a country's economic conditions, the development of its financial institutions and financial markets, financial inclusion, investor behavior, financial policy, and the regulation of investors.

The main bond investors in major developed economies are institutional investors, and different institutions are motivated by different factors. In the case of banks, asset management tools and regulatory factors are the main factors related to bond investment. In addition to lending, banks pursue strategies to increase their profits by holding various investment assets. Bond investments are utilized as one of the main targets for such asset management. In addition, in response to the recent tightening of regulations on bank liquidity, banks are expanding their investments in government bonds having high credit quality and liquidity.[6]

Insurance companies and pension funds hold long-term bonds to match their long-term liabilities. As the demand for these long-term investments increases, countries with developed insurance and pension industries tend to have increasing shares of investment in long-term government and corporate bonds.

In developed economies, central banks tend to invest primarily in government-issued securities. Since the global financial crisis, the monetary policy of major central banks has shifted from its traditional role of fighting inflation to that of stabilizing the financial markets. This shift in monetary policy objectives has led central banks to cut policy rates and purchase government bonds issued by governments to finance fiscal policy.

6 Basel III introduced regulations on banks' liquidity coverage ratios, which require banks to hold more liquid assets than their expected net cash outflows over a 30-day period. In response to these regulations, banks have been expanding their investments in government bonds, which are a typical liquid asset.

In major developed countries, foreign securities have constituted a significant portion of portfolio investments. This is largely due to the increase in financial globalization and investment strategies aimed at achieving risk diversification. This increase in foreign ownership of bonds has two sides to it. On the positive side, it broadens the investor base, thereby increasing the depth and breadth of the bond market. From the issuer's perspective, this broadening of the bond investor base benefits issuers by reducing financing costs and allowing them to issue bonds with more favorable terms. On the other hand, if the share of foreign investors exceeds a certain level, the inflow and outflow of foreign funds may increase, heightening the risk of financial instability.

Retail Investor Base

For the development of the bond market, various types of bond investors must be fostered, and retail investors are an important source of investment in bonds. For these reasons, some developed economies are pursuing policies to broaden their bases of retail investors by introducing sovereign bonds.

A desirable market structure is one in which the system for protecting retail investors is functioning properly, so that retail investors have high confidence in the bond market and account for a certain proportion of that market. To achieve this, there needs to be a legal basis ensuring that investors' investments are kept safe and used for investment despite any failure of an investment intermediary, as well as a system to protect investors. It is also important for retail investors to invest actively in and maintain certain shares of investment in bonds.

Foreign Investor Base

Foreign investors invest in government bonds in various countries. For example, they own 30% of US government bonds, around 20% of the Republic of Korea government bonds, and more than 10% of Japanese government bonds.

The benefit of an increase in foreign investment in the bond markets is ambiguous, however. On the one hand, increased foreign investment in bonds has the positive effect of broadening the demand base in the host country's bond market and improving its market efficiency. On the other hand, increased volatility in short-term foreign investments can have a negative impact on exchange rates, constrain monetary policy, and lead to increased financial instability as funds flow in and out of the country. Nevertheless, efforts to improve market conditions for expanding foreign investment are crucial, as a certain level of foreign investment in the local bond market has a positive impact on promoting the development of the bond market and broadening the demand base.

Investor Protection

Customer deposits are funds deposited by investment clients with securities firms for the purpose of purchasing and selling securities. In general, there is an information asymmetry between securities firms and their customers, which can lead to moral hazard problems in which investors leave cash in their securities accounts, and securities firms misappropriate those funds, as well as limitations in protecting customer property in the event of a securities firm's insolvency. Therefore, measures need to be taken to strengthen investor protection by establishing separate accounts for customer deposits, either by setting up a dedicated deposit system or by separating customer deposits from those of the securities firms.

The segregation of customer deposits is a practice that aims to separate and safeguard customer funds from risks arising from the purchase and sale of securities, and even in developed countries, the complete separation of customer funds from those of the securities companies is at the core of the customer deposit protection system. The ideal situation is one in which the system for protecting retail investors is functioning properly, ensuring that, despite any failure of an intermediary, the investor's funds are kept safe and can be used for investment, and the legal basis for investor protection is in place.

Issuer Base

Benchmarks

Bonds serve as a long-term financing tool for sovereigns, corporations, and financial institutions. To create conditions for issuers to raise funds through bonds, among various sources of financing, a market structure that meets the needs of issuers must be introduced.

In addition to its role in efficiently financing the government, the government bond market also serves as a benchmark for the broader bond market. Subject to their maintaining adequate fiscal prudence, governments can issue government bonds to stimulate the bond market and raise funds for fiscal expenditures. Accordingly, countries with efficient government bond issuance systems are characterized by having a high share of bonds in their government borrowing.

In the private sector, bond issuance is a crucial means for companies to raise necessary capital, and successful bond issuance can simultaneously be used as an opportunity for the company's value to be reevaluated in the financial market. However, in the absence of a developed corporate bond market, issuers are forced to rely on banks for most of their financing, which limits their abilities to organize optimal capital and debt structures and may lead to financing inefficiencies.

Therefore, policies to vitalize the bond market are an important factor in supporting economic growth and promoting industrial diversification, in addition to expanding sources of financing for companies and financial institutions. To create an environment that enables issuers (governments, financial institutions, corporations) to make informed decisions about raising funds through bonds, among various financing instruments, a market structure that meets their needs must be in place. Bonds must have advantages over other sources of financing in terms of tenor, size, convenience, and cost in order to be considered for financing. Therefore, it is important to create a market structure that benefits issuers.

Securitization

A securitization is a financial investment vehicle that raises funds by issuing securities backed by assets. Typical types of securitizations are mortgage-backed securities, which are backed by mortgages, and asset-backed securities, which are backed by assets other than mortgages. To issue an asset-backed or mortgage-backed security, a group of assets is transferred or entrusted to a special-purpose vehicle established for the purpose of securitization, and the special-purpose vehicle issues securities based on the cash flows of the transferred assets. After issuing the asset-back security, the servicer uses the cash flows from the assets to redeem the security. For such securitization to occur smoothly, a system that accurately defines and regulates the concept, procedures, and legal issues associated with securitization must be introduced.

Securitization has several advantages. First, it has the effect of reducing the financing costs of enterprises and financial institutions through the issuance of high-credit quality securities. Second, securitization performs the function of transferring credit risk and can provide off-balance financing to improve the capital adequacy of financial institutions. Third, securitization plays a role in expanding the supply of highly creditworthy securities to investors, thereby providing credibility to bonds.

On the other hand, if credit risk is transferred using securitization techniques without an appropriate regulatory framework, it may give rise to systemic risk. Prior to the global financial crisis, securitization based on subprime mortgages and products such as collateralized debt obligations were widely used. As securitizations based on these subprime mortgages expanded, originators used the proceeds to originate new subprime mortgages, and the process was repeated, resulting in the transfer of the distressed assets to a wide variety of investors. Subsequently, as the delinquency rate of subprime mortgages increased due to concerns about the economic downturn and rising interest rates, the assets underlying the securitizations became insolvent, leading to losses for investors, which were major factors leading to the global financial crisis. In the absence of an appropriate regulatory system, excessive expansion of securitization may contribute to financial market instability and increased systemic risk. Therefore, the establishment of an appropriate regulatory system and disclosure system is crucial for the success of the securitization system.

Credit Assessment

Due to the information asymmetry between borrowers and lenders in the bond market, the appropriate and continuous disclosure of bond issuer information must be institutionalized. Unlike the case of loans, bond investors are composed of various types of investors with diverse investment objectives, and therefore, information about an issuer's creditworthiness must be provided to market participants in an equal and fair manner.

In the corporate bond market, credit rating agencies play a role in bridging the information asymmetry between issuers and investors. For corporate bonds issued in a public offering, investors typically demand a credit rating. This is because investors have investment criteria that only allow them to invest in bonds with certain credit ratings. As a result, most corporate bonds are rated by reputable rating agencies before being issued.

Credit rating is a system that provides stakeholders such as investors and financial institutions with a certain symbol, or credit rating, after analyzing the likelihood that the principal of a specific security or a specific debt will be repaid according to the terms of issuance, based on factors affecting repayment. The credit ratings comprise mainly issuer ratings and issue ratings. The credit rating of a bond is a method of expressing the likelihood of its repayment by assessing the creditworthiness of the issuer and the characteristics of the issued security. The issuer rating assesses the overall creditworthiness of the issuer, evaluating its ability to repay external debt based on a comprehensive analysis of its financial situation. An issuer rating assesses the issuer's overall creditworthiness and ability to repay debt based on its financial analysis. This rating serves as the foundation for deriving the issue credit rating, which is determined by adjusting the issuer rating up or down based on specific conditions of the issued security, such as guarantees, collateral, seniority, or subordination. Credit ratings perform the function of providing information to reduce the information asymmetry between investors and issuers. They also play a role in enhancing market efficiency by helping to determine appropriate pricing reflective of risk levels based on credit ratings.

Intermediation

Secondary Market Structure

The secondary bond market is a market that serves to enhance the liquidity of bonds, where bond prices are formed based on market principles. The establishment of an efficient secondary market is the basis for the vitalization of the primary bond market. A well-functioning secondary market also boosts the liquidity of bonds, improves the completeness of the yield curve, and enhances the overall health of the financial markets.

In view of all this, major countries devote varied efforts to building efficient and transparent secondary markets. Secondary bond markets in major countries differ somewhat from country to country. In most countries, the secondary market is primarily based on the over-the-counter market, as bond trading is conducted mainly by institutional investors and brokers. However, some countries have introduced bond trading systems on their local stock exchanges.

The degree of secondary market activity can be assessed by comparing liquidity indicators across bond types. Additionally, the appropriateness of the secondary market system and the trading methods for each bond type can be evaluated. In general, standardized government bonds are more liquid, while corporate bonds are relatively less liquid.

Bond Trading Businesses

The role of trading firms and trading platforms in connecting issuers and investors is also important. Bond trading firms can be defined as financial institutions that act as underwriters in the primary market and as dealers and brokers in the secondary market. Bond trading companies play a crucial role in establishing a fair and transparent pricing system for bonds, enhancing market transparency, and developing a market infrastructure that meets the needs of both investors and issuers.

The financial institutions that can trade bonds vary somewhat from country to country. Some countries have introduced systems where only investment companies (securities companies) play a role in bond trading, while others allow banks to participate in bond trading as well. There are also differences in how bond trading works for various types of bonds. In the case of government bonds, most countries have adopted the primary dealer system, which gives primary dealers a monopoly in underwriting government bonds and imposes obligations on them to strengthen activity in the secondary market. The qualifications, functions, and roles of primary dealers vary depending on the characteristics of the different countries. Therefore, in order for developing countries to develop their bond markets, they must define and develop the role of market participants appropriately so as to reflect the role and status of their financial institutions.

Transparency of Trading and Pricing

The International Organization of Securities Commissioners has published proposals for enhancing corporate bond transparency (2004), a study on enhancing liquidity in the corporate bond secondary market (2017), and proposals for enhancing corporate bond reporting obligations and transparency (2017). These guidelines recommend enhancing conditions related to four types of information, in order to improve market transparency.

First, investors should strive to acquire the necessary information to trade bonds, enabling a deeper understanding and more effective monitoring of the bond market.

Second, to facilitate the acquisition of bond market information, it is necessary to establish a reporting system, standardize reporting methods, and ensure transparency.

Third, supervisory authorities should enhance their acquisition of pre-trade information to bolster market harmonization, including ensuring effective market monitoring, market integration, and the fairness of transactions.

Fourth, transaction information in the bond secondary market should be reported to supervisors to support effective supervision. Proactive and reactive transparency in the secondary bond market is expected to promote efficient bond pricing, investor protection, and market vitalization by enhancing stakeholders' confidence in the bond market. To improve transparency in secondary market transactions, it is essential to introduce market conditions in which transaction-related information is adequately provided to stakeholders ex ante and ex post, prices are determined based on information appropriate to market conditions, and regulation is based on market monitoring by regulators.

REFERENCES

Asian Development Bank (ADB). 2019. *Good Practices for Developing a Local Currency Bond Market: Lessons from the ASEAN+3 Asia Bond Market Initiative.*

———. 2021. *Supporting Capital Market Development and Reform in Developing Asia (Phase 1).*

———. 2022. *Collective Investment Scheme Transactions in ASEAN+3.*

———. 2023. *Local Currency Bond Market Development and Currency Stability amid Market Turmoil.*

B. Eschweiler. 2006. *Bond Market Regulation and Supervision in Asia.* BIS Papers No. 30.

International Monetary Fund (IMF) and World Bank. 2001. *Developing Government Bond Markets: A Handbook.*

———. 2020. *Local Currency Bond Markets Law Reform.*

———. 2021. *Guidance Notes for Developing Government Local Currency Bond Markets.*

International Organization of Securities Commissions (IOSCO). 2003. *Objectives and Principles of Securities Regulation.*

———. 2017a. *Methodology for Assessing Implementation of the IOSCO Objectives and Principles of Securities Regulation.*

———. 2017b. *Regulatory Reporting and Public Transparency in the Secondary Corporate Bond Markets.*

United States Agency for International Development. 2010. *Developing Government Bond Markets: Primer, Diagnostic Checklist, and Guideline for Preparing a Model Scope of Work.*

World Bank, IMF, European Bank, and Organisation for Economic Co-operation and Development. 2013. *Local Currency Bond Markets: A Diagnostic Framework.*

www.ingramcontent.com/pod-product-compliance
Lightning Source LLC
Chambersburg PA
CBHW041758220926
51847CB00014B/241
* 9 7 8 9 2 9 2 7 7 6 3 2 9 *